WOMEN *of* GREAT FAITH

EMBRACE YOUR DIVINE IDENTITY AS A DAUGHTER OF A KING & A MOTHER IN ZION

WOMEN *of* GREAT FAITH

EMBRACE YOUR DIVINE IDENTITY AS A DAUGHTER OF A KING & A MOTHER IN ZION

Michelle Grant

CFI
An imprint of Cedar Fort, Inc.
Springville, Utah

Paperback ISBN 13: 978-1-4621-5019-9
eBook ISBN 13: 978-1-4621-5020-5

Published by CFI, an imprint of Cedar Fort, Inc.
2373 W. 700 S., Suite 100, Springville, UT 84663
Distributed by Cedar Fort, Inc., www.cedarfort.com

Library of Congress Cataloging Number: 2025946068

Cover design by Shawnda Craig

Printed in the United States of America

10 9 8 7 6 5 4 3 2 1

Printed on acid-free paper

This book has been a labour of love and five years in the making. I have poured my testimony and soul into the words on these pages. I know that there is great truth in them. I know that Father in Heaven has prompted me to put these thoughts into a book to help my many beautiful sisters all over the world.

I would like to dedicate this book to my children and grandchildren. I have been blessed to be a mother and grandmother in mortality and have these incredible spirits enrich our home. They are my inspiration and my greatest joy. They have taught me far more than I could ever have taught them. Rebekah, Matthew, Jacob, Amber, James, Luke, Abigail, Elena, Jaco, Samuel, Blueberry, Niko, Finley & Bertie.

I would also like to dedicate this book to the women who have helped me become who I am. My mum, mother-in-law, grandmothers, aunts, sisters, sisters-in-laws, and friends. My ultimate cheer squad!

Finally, it is dedicated to my husband, who has been my biggest support and helped me believe in my worth and develop my knowledge that I am a woman of great faith.

But, most of all, the dedication goes to YOU, as I wrote it just for you.

Contents

"Each of His daughters has been taught and prepared and gifted premortally with marvelous potential to become a queen in the celestial kingdom."[1]

1. Jean B. Bingham, "Extraordinary Daughters of God," *Liahona*, Mar. 2020.

Introduction

We can all think of amazing and incredible women who literally change the world and the people around them—women who influence for good and are natural nurturers of everyone they meet. There is a catalogue of women who have changed history and have made such a difference; their impact has been felt and will continue to be felt throughout all generations and time.

Each of us will be acquainted with individuals within our own family or friendship group that really stand out—incredible examples of daughters of a King and mothers in Zion. Many of us aspire to be like these women, believing that they are better than us, that they are greater because they have more talent, skills, and capacity than we deem ourselves to have. They are more, and we can only dream about being like them.

Just Stop It!

I want you to know right now: YOU ARE TOTALLY WRONG! In this book we will explore YOU and how you might reach YOUR potential and believe in YOURSELF as a precious and beautiful daughter of a King and a mother in Zion.

Regardless of your age, status, and personal circumstances, you need to know that you have so much greatness within you. You are a child of God and an heir, even a joint heir with Jesus Christ (see Romans 8:17). Father sent us each here to Earth with different skills, attributes, and spiritual gifts; however, He DID NOT send us here without the ability to be great; He endowed you with this ability in great abundance. He looked at His plan for the world and knew that it needed you, the exact you that Father dearly loved and cherished in the premortal realm and has done for eternity. He knew then and knows now of your potential and how you will change the world. You were born for greatness and to play a magnificent part in His plan, and being here, right here, today was the plan the Father made; your existence is not incidental or insignificant. It is fundamental and key in the Plan of Happiness. Digest that and don't ever forget it.

Come along with us on this beautiful journey of discovery as we each better realise our potential and begin to see ourselves more like our Father in Heaven sees us—wonderfully and totally incredible. My hope is that this book will become a cheerleader and friend, a loving message from one sister to another.

FAQs: Forever Asking Questions!

Do you feel sometimes that the record is stuck, that time and time again we ask the same questions, often receiving the same answers, but somehow we don't really hear them? Or do we not believe that we are enough or able to achieve what the answer portrays? Maybe we don't understand them. Or we don't want to understand them. So let's start out with the basic questions, the ones that lie deep within each of our hearts and souls. But this time, can we listen, really listen? The answers to these basic questions are for you, and I want you to listen and really believe them. Embrace them in your heart and let your soul rejoice as it recognises heavenly truths.

Where Do I Start?

"The journey of a thousand miles begins with a single step."[2]

A journey of any kind is strewn with questions, and discovering your potential is no different. The questions and answers are the building blocks of your greatness and the foundation to the faith and belief that you need to have in yourself. It is also important to remember that believing in yourself is essential, and when I find that hard and think I am not good enough, I remember, Heavenly Father thinks

2. Lao Tzu, *Tao Te Ching*, chapter 64.

I am. He thinks that I can do this; in fact, He KNOWS that I can do it. Putting my faith in His faith in me gives me additional strength and perspective.

"When you climb up a ladder, you must begin at the bottom, and ascend step by step, until you arrive at the top; and so it is with the principles of the gospel—you must begin with the first, and go on until you learn all the principles of exaltation."[3]

Learning about who we are and gaining a testimony goes hand in hand with learning our true worth and potential as woman of great faith. The fact that you are here, right now, reading this book means that you have already started your journey.

Who Am I?

President Dallin H. Oaks teaches us: "Consider the power of the idea taught in our beloved song 'I Am a Child of God' (*Hymns*, 1985, 301) . . . Here is the answer to one of life's great questions, 'Who am I?' I am a child of God with a spirit lineage to heavenly parents. That parentage defines our eternal potential. That powerful idea is a potent antidepressant. It can strengthen each of us to make righteous choices and to seek the best that is within us."[4]

> You are a daughter of devoted heavenly parents, a loving Father and Mother; you were infinitely precious to Them in the beginning and still are. The distance we have between us only makes Them love us more and yearn for us to one day be home with Them again in Their perfect embrace. You, like me, were faithful to Father and His plan for our progression through mortality and beyond. You are a beloved little sister to Jesus Christ; He is your elder brother, your Saviour and protector. When He came to Earth, He atoned for you. He played His part in the plan of salvation because He loves you so much. You are a Heavenly spirit on a mortal journey with all its challenges and trials—the ups and downs of mortality. You knew when Father sent you here that these were the conditions, and you

3. *Teachings of Presidents of the Church: Joseph Smith* [1976], 268; see also 221.
4. Dallin H. Oaks, "Powerful Ideas," *Ensign*, Nov. 1995, 25.

> wanted to come; in fact, I believe that we jumped for joy and were filled with excitement as Father told each of us individually that it was our turn. I like to think that He took time with us to help prepare us, maybe giving a father's blessing, and embraced us. We knew it was part of our journey to greatness so that we could be more like Father and Mother. You have within you the ability and capability to be so much more that you realise. He sees your eternal and celestial potential, and He knows that you can make it. You are His.

Why Am I Here?

You are here, firstly, to gain a physical body just like Heavenly Father and Mother. You are here to learn, grow, and develop. You are here to experience the joys and pains of mortality and to spread your wings and fly. You are here because this is when Father needed you, to play your crucial part in His marvelous plan, not by accident but by divine design. You are here to fulfil His plan and to make a difference to so many people. You are here to learn about yourself and how incredible you are. Most of all, you bring with you a little bit of heaven.

"You were chosen *not* for your bodily characteristics but for your *spiritual* attributes, such as bravery, courage, integrity of heart, a thirst for truth, a hunger for wisdom, and a desire to serve others."[5]

What Are You Doing?

This is a question only you can answer. Hopefully you are doing your best. Hopefully you get up each time you fall and you fall to your knees for forgiveness each time you stumble. Elder Dieter F. Uchtdorf teaches us that

> It can be discouraging at times to know what it means to be a [child] of God and yet come up short. The adversary likes to take advantage of these feelings. Satan would rather that you define

5. Russell M. Nelson, "Decisions for Eternity," *Ensign* or *Liahona*, Nov. 2013, 107.

yourself by your sins instead of your divine potential. [Sisters], don't listen to him.

We have all seen a toddler learn to walk. He takes a small step and totters. He falls. Do we scold such an attempt? Of course not. What father would punish a toddler for stumbling? We encourage, we applaud, and we praise because with every small step, the child is becoming more like his parents.

Now, [sisters], compared to the perfection of God, we mortals are scarcely more than awkward, faltering toddlers. But our loving Heavenly Father wants us to become more like Him, and, dear [sisters], that should be our eternal goal too. God understands that we get there not in an instant but by taking one step at a time.[6]

"Of all the creations of the Almighty, there is none more beautiful, none more inspiring than a lovely daughter of God who walks in virtue with an understanding of why she should do so, who honors and respects her body as a thing sacred and divine, who cultivates her mind and constantly enlarges the horizon of her understanding, who nurtures her spirit with everlasting truth."[7]

This part of the plan and our time on Earth is for us to grow, to learn, and to become more like Father and Mother. Do not be overwhelmed. We are told that we will do these things "Line upon Line . . . here a little and there a little" (2 Nephi 28:30), just the same way an infant learns to talk and walk. Father knew that we would find it hard and that we would make mistakes; He loves us regardless of our biggest error or greatest failing. He wants your mortal experience to be amazing and for you to understand and fully appreciate your potential. He wants your life to be full of events, and they may include marriage and motherhood, or they may not; regardless of whether they do or do not, that in no way changes or reduces your worth or potential. You came to Earth for your own unique journey and adventure; comparing life is not the way to benchmark yourself. There are

6. Dieter F. Uchtdorf, "Four Titles," *Ensign* or *Liahona*, May 2013, 58.

7. Gordon B. Hinckley, "Our Responsibility to Our Young Women," *Ensign*, Sept. 1988, 11.

only two people we should compare ourselves to: 1) Ourselves—are we better today than we were yesterday? Or are we trying to do better tomorrow than we did today? 2) Our older brother and Saviour Jesus Christ, who we want to try to become a little more like through our life's journey. However, don't ever forget that comparison is the ultimate thief of all joy; celebrate your progress (and that of others) no matter how little or seemingly insignificant you might think it is.

Where Am I Going?

We are not talking about your destination bucket list and where your next holiday destination is, although exploring this wonderful world that Father gave us is an amazing bonus in this mortal journey. You chose where you were going an eternity ago, at the dawn of time, when you chose to follow Father's plan. You chose the celestial kingdom, so that is where you are going. Let's just say that again, and really take it in. You are going to the celestial kingdom, as long as you continue to choose to; plan and prepare by doing the things required to go there. You are going to be part of a perfect eternal family, and again, your choices here on Earth will impact how that family looks. You are going to be an eternal being; you are going to die, and you are going to be resurrected. There is so much more in this plan than just the mortal experience, and we need to plan where we are going whilst we are here right now. Church, Relief Society, temple attendance, and other positive pursuits can help us keep our eyes firmly fixed on the true and most amazing destination of celestial glory. The important thing is that we are going forward, going the right direction, and that we have a plan. Whatever you do, don't just tread water or turn away from the light.

Elder Bruce R. McConkie declared, "Good and faithful members of the Church will be saved, even though they are far from perfect in this life."[8]

---

8. Bruce R. McConkie, "The Seven Deadly Heresies," BYU devotional, June 1, 1980, speeches.byu.edu.

Will I Ever Reach My Potential?

Elder Dieter F. Uchtdorf taught: "We were His children before we came to this world, and we will be His children forevermore. This basic truth should change the way we look at ourselves, our brothers and sisters, and life itself."[9]

Father has total faith in you and your ability to make it home to Him. If we were able to see ourselves as Father or our Saviour does, we would have more confidence, more faith in our abilities, more drive, more compassion for ourselves, more hope, and our lives would be filled with so much more joy. We have the horrid habit of looking in the mirror with mortal eyes and judging ourselves with a mortal mind; this is not the way to achieve greatness but the way to let the natural man hold us back. We need to remember that this mortal body doesn't control things; it is, however, a temple for our spirit to dwell in during mortality—a temple just as beautiful, precious, and important as those that dot the earth. We need to look back in that mirror with spiritual eyes, remembering that the person looking back at us is precious to our Father, that our bodies were designed and created by Him. He chose and believed that this person was essential to His plan, and when He looked at the world, He knew it needed one of you! There is only one of you, and that was the point and the plan. Remember that. Without you being you, the best version of you, the puzzle is incomplete.

You are loved. You need to remind yourself every day. Pop a sticky note on your mirror so you can see it and be reminded to love yourself. True self-love is part of Father's plan too. He taught us in Matthew 22:39, "Thou shalt love thy neighbour as thyself." He commanded that we love ourselves because we are one of His incredible creations. He took time and care to make you the way you are, so embrace it—grow and improve yourself, by all means, but don't ever stop loving and caring for yourself as He told you to.

---

9. Dieter F. Uchtdorf, "Four Titles," 58.

Who Will I Become?

This is what we hope you will decide and work out as you read, study, reflect on, and embrace this book. We will explore and discover your potential and help you set goals. Don't be overwhelmed here; you are growing always. You will not be able to reach your true potential today, tomorrow, or even next year, BUT you will get there, climbing the ladder one rung at a time. You can look back and see how far you have come, but keep looking ahead with heaven in mind; this will always help you see that you have so much more potential, greatness, and incredible times and experiences than where you stand today. President Nelson has told us many times that "The best is yet to come!"[10] This is the same for all of us. Remember that each of us is climbing our very own ladder and having our own struggles, but don't ever forget that each rung is one step closer to your goal, one step closer to perfection, and one step closer to heaven, even if they all still seem so far away.

The reality is you are a daughter of a King, a beloved daughter of our Father in Heaven; you are His, and you are precious. You are a mother in Zion, and through mortality you will be able to nurture and help develop many of Father's other children. "Remember the worth of souls is great in the sight of God" (Doctrine and Covenants 18:10); that includes your soul too. These things will not change; however, you will become more. You are already enough, but you can be so much more. He invites us to "come unto Christ, and be perfected in Him" (Moroni 10:32). We can become perfected, we can become like our Saviour Jesus Christ and like Heavenly Father and Mother.

President Joseph Smith taught us, "If men do not comprehend the character of God, they do not comprehend themselves. . . . God Himself was once as we are now, and is an exalted man, and sits enthroned in yonder heavens!"[11]

We can become goddesses; we are "joint-heirs with Christ" (Romans 8:17) and can inherit all that the Father has—all of it—not some of it, and not one of us here on Earth is more able or entitled

---

10. Russell M. Nelson, "The Lord Jesus Christ Will Come Again, Oct. 2024, 122.

11. *Teachings: Joseph Smith*, 40.

that you. We are equal. Those of us who choose to be obedient and receive the full blessings of the Saviour's incredible Atonement will inherit all that the Father has (see Romans 8:14–18; Galatians 3:26–29; Doctrine and Covenants 84:38). He has told us what we have the potential to become, one step at a time, with the incredible support and grace of our Saviour Jesus Christ. If we could even glimpse it in our minds, it would seem impossible, but He has told us that it is possible for each and every one of us. What amazing potential you have! You need to know it, believe it, and then act on it. Your true potential is there waiting for you to unleash it. It's not going to be easy, but He has promised that it will all be worth it!

Planning: Five Steps to Greatness

We have discussed that just as we climb a ladder one rung at a time, reaching our ultimate greatness is something we do one step at a time. The steps to achieve your goals will require planning and the utilisation of your many skills; they won't happen by accident! So, before we start our journey, let's get together some weapons in our armoury to ensure that we are triumphant in our quest.

Step One: Focus

"Keep your thoughts positive because your thoughts become your words. Keep your words positive because your words become your behaviour. Keep your behaviour positive because your behaviour becomes your habits. Keep your habits positive because your habits become your values. Keep your values positive because your values become your destiny."[12]

In all endeavours we need to keep our eye on the prize: eternal life surrounded by those we love. Having eternal focus will help us stay on track. What can seem like tiny millimeters off course during a lifetime will take you miles from your destination. President Dieter F. Uchtdorf taught us that

12. Attributed to Mahatma Gandhi.

"The difference between happiness and misery . . . often comes down to an error of only a few degrees."[13]

He went on to teach about the tragedy of a flight crashing into an unexpected volcano because the coordinates had been changed by only two degrees. The flight was twenty-eight miles off course and crashed into the volcano covered in snow, losing all the passengers on board.

"It was a terrible tragedy brought on by a minor error— a matter of only a few degrees."[14]

Being just a couple of degrees off course could change your destination completely, with eternal consequences. You could end up miles and miles from your expected destination. Setting our focus and keeping it on our direct path is essential. We need to stay focused and committed to the destination; we can sit and rest from time to time, but we should not depart from the path, even the slightest. If things transpire against our plan and we take a temporary deviation, we can reset our course using the Atonement of Jesus Christ, embracing His endless and infinite love.

We need to stay positive. One challenge with a long-term goal is that it can be hard to stay focused and on task when the result seems so far away. You may be able to relate to this hardship during a weight-loss journey. We have the goal, and we set out with enthusiasm, but after a few weeks the weight loss slows down or even stalls and we quickly fall back into the poor habits that may have contributed to our excess weight in the beginning. We need to stay positive and focused even during the hard times. We need to not be scared to ask for help, and we need to always seek out the silver linings in the clouds and look for rainbows in the rain.

"Life isn't about waiting for the storm to pass. It's about learning how to dance in the rain."[15]

---

13. Dieter F. Uchtdorf, "A Matter of a Few Degrees," *Liahona*, Apr. 2008, 57, 58.

14. Dieter F. Uchtdorf, "A Few Degrees," 58.

15. Attributed to Vivian Greene.

Mental or physical mood boards can be a great way of focusing and looking at the bigger picture. Consider the following as you create your mood board:

- How does your eternal home look to you?
- Your loved ones and friends will probably be the first people you imagine being there with you; list them.
- What goals do you need to set in your life to ensure that you can take your place there? It can help you focus on where you want to be but also why you want to be there.
- When you think of a heavenly existence in celestial glory, which specific people will help make it heaven?
- When you think of these beloved individuals, consider how you might best invite them to come along with you on this eternal journey.

Having the focus and the goals and understanding the whos and the whys will help us live today with more direction as we seek to fulfil our potential. Creating a board can be such great fun, like creating a collage of your mind and your dreams; many people assemble photos, images, colour palettes, textures, fabrics, and other sensory elements that showcase their goals and desires—some people do this by scrap-booking, others by using digital media, and others a Pinterest board.

Focus is necessary in our journey, and there is one motivation that should be a priority for all Latter-day Saint women. Sister Sydney Smith Reynolds wrote:

> Our primary concerns must be these: Do I know that Jesus is the Christ, the literal Son of God? Do I believe and follow the words of the living prophets? How do I respond to the challenges of daily life? Am I usually trying to please the Lord, other people, or myself? (Sydney Smith Reynolds, "A Mother's Commission," *Ensign*, Mar. 1984)

You could ask yourself, *How would I live differently if my focus was on pleasing the Lord rather than on pleasing others or myself?*

Where is your focus? Do you need to adjust the direction of your journey by a degree or two? Can you help those whom you may have influence over adjust theirs too? What three things do you feel you need to give additional focus to over the next few months as you take this journey through the book with us and establish yourself as the Lord already sees you—a beautiful, wonderful woman of great faith?

Step Two: Plan

Coming to Earth was all a part of Father's plan. When we agreed to mortality and its many wondrous experiences, it was a part of that very plan. Where we are all going is also part of His plan, the most beautiful plan in the plan of happiness or salvation. This teaches us that Father is a planner. He doesn't just take things by chance or accident. He is methodical, and His plans have an eternal structure. We can implement structuring methods in our lives to set plans in place as a way to achieve our full potential. In *Alice's Adventures in Wonderland*, the Cheshire Cat and Alice have an interesting exchange:

> "Would you tell me, please, which way I ought to go from here?"
> "That depends a good deal on where you want to get to," said the Cat.
> "I don't much care where—" said Alice.
> "Then it doesn't matter which way you go," said the Cat.
> "—so long as I get *somewhere*," Alice added as an explanation.
> "Oh, you're sure to do that," said the Cat, "if you only walk long enough."[16]

We might feel like Alice seeking and looking for someone to lay out our mortal journey for us with a full plan of the road trip, tell us what to do next or where to go, what stops we should make, and details of the best things to look out for—a kind of mortal tour guide. The good news is that unlike the Cheshire Cat, we have the very person who sent us here to start with just at the end of a prayer: our beloved guide, our Father in Heaven. We also benefit from the great wisdom and experience of an elder brother to help direct us, the Holy Ghost to prompt us along the way, the scriptures, and modern-day prophets and revelation. We do not rely on the Cheshire Cat! However, we need to decide on our plan and think about our first steps and where we are going. If we ask Him without knowing where we want to be,

16. Lewis Carroll, *Alice's Adventures in Wonderland*, Project Gutenberg.

His direction will be hard for us to follow. If we ask for specific help having used our own wisdom to work it out in our minds first, then the directions will be easier to follow.

Father wanted to bless us further during our mortal journey and planned for patriarchal blessings as personal passages of sacred scripture just for us, to give us some personal and specific outlines for our eternal life and help us plan and choose our direction. Have you received yours? If so, when did you last look at it? You could make a photocopy and keep it in your scriptures or on your phone where you can read it regularly. Take time to study it. What does Father have planned for you? What can you achieve? What do you need to work on? What do you need to avoid? What are the special gifts He has given you? We are repeatedly reminded that we all have much to learn from our own personal scripture and that we should give heed and, as President Thomas S. Monson has said:

> Study it carefully. Be guided by its cautions. Live to merit its promises. If you have not yet received your patriarchal blessing, plan for the time when you will receive it, and then cherish it.[17]

When making your plans (yes, there will be more than one), focus on what is important to you. Taking a little bit of time to plan will allow space in your life for all the details. There is a story about a jar, which was shared with me in a lesson in my youth—many of you will be familiar with it.

A teacher presented a large jar, which she filled with golf balls. She then asked the class, "Is this full?" To which they confidently replied, "Yes!" She then rummaged in a bag and produced a bag of small pebbles and poured them into the jar. "Is it full now?" "Yes," they replied tentatively. She then pulled out a bag of sand and poured it in between the stones and golf balls. "Is it full now?" No one wanted to reply, as they were now not sure. She then pulled out a bottle of water and filled up the jar.

This story is perfect to teach us about the importance of planning. The teacher could not have gotten all the items into the jar had she

---

17. Thomas S. Monson, "May You Have Courage," *Ensign* or *Liahona*, May 2009, 125–26.

chosen a different order, but when things were done in the right order, they all fit.

The golf balls represent the most important things—for example, family, the gospel, health, friends, and passions. Get them in first. The pebbles come next—these might include a job, a place to live, or a car. The sand represents the smaller stuff. The water proves that even when you have gotten everything else in, there is still room to relax! For me, the water represents a lovely, big bubble bath. You and only you choose what are golf balls and what is sand for you, but if you make a plan, you have the best hope of fitting it all in.

"If you fail to plan, you are planning to fail."[18]

"If ye are prepared ye shall not fear" (Doctrine and Covenants 38:30). Make a time to plan. Choose a time—for me, Sunday evening works well—when you can compile your schedule; ensure that you make room for all the important stuff, like home evening, *Come, Follow Me* study, and prayer (individually and as a family). Schedule time for the temple and to minister to those you have been assigned to care for. If it is on the schedule, it is more likely to happen. Whatever you do, be realistic. Don't set yourself up for failure by overloading yourself or your family. Life is to be enjoyed, not endured. Find joy and success in your accomplishments, and remember the things that worked well whilst readjusting and resetting the things that were missed or overlooked in previous weeks. Life sometimes really does just get in the way of even our best-laid plans.

What have you learned from your patriarchal blessing? What do you need to work on? What do you need to plan for?

Take time to think about the story of the jar. List your:

- Golf balls
- Small pebbles
- Sand
- Water

18. Author unknown.

Do you need to adjust what are golf balls and what is sand so that you can achieve all that you want to and all that Father might want you to?

Step Three: Set Goals

"[Satan] knows he can't improve, he can't progress, that worlds without end he will never have a bright tomorrow. He is a miserable man bound by eternal limitations, and he wants you to be miserable too. Well, don't fall for that."[19]

It is essential that we plan to ensure that we keep on task, by setting specific goals that are short and also longer term; doing this will enable us to grow in our potential but also in joy.

> What do you want to accomplish in your life? What are your goals and aspirations? If your long-term goal is to enter the Celestial Kingdom to live forever with our Heavenly Parents and with loved family members, that singular focus will take you farther than you now think is possible (see 1 Corinthians 2:9).[20]

We are all familiar with New Year's and the endless list of goals or resolutions we burden ourselves with: list after list of unrealistic ideals. We start with gusto and passion, and within a few weeks, they disappear one by one. "I will try again next year" is our mantra.

Children and youth in the Church have been taught the importance of setting goals to help in their journey of personal development, teaching skills and habits that they can learn and utilise. This will enable them be better at setting and accomplishing goals. They are also taught that goals need to be set for the right reasons and that they need to be planned out and then regularly reviewed. There is nothing wrong with adjusting your plan or goal as you move forward to ensure you can achieve it. Rather than give up and fail, revise your plan.

When setting goals, consider:

---

19. Jeffrey R. Holland, "Tomorrow the Lord Will Do Wonders among You," *Ensign* or *Liahona*, Apr. 2016, 125.

20. Jean B. Bingham, "Extraordinary Daughters of God," *Liahona*, Mar. 2020, from BYU Women's Conference address, May 5, 2017.

- **What are your goals?** Write them down and put them somewhere you can be reminded of them every day. Putting pen to paper makes them real. The more you see and are reminded of your goals, the better chance you have of keeping on task and achieving them. Make yourself accountable where possible; talk about them with family and other loved ones who can support you.
- **Get to the point!** Be specific. Generic goals, like "Learn to play the piano" have no guidelines or limits, so you need to include what and when. Are you taking lessons? What pieces of music do you want to play? How and when are you going to do it? Are there mini goals within a larger goal? Be specific and be realistic; the more details you have, the easier it will be to follow the goal planned out in your mind.
- **Set mini goals.** Whatever goals you set for yourself, make sure you have lots of mini goals or markers along the way to "tick off" to show your progress. If you want to run a marathon, that's a big goal, but maybe you could plan to run a mile, then five, and work your way up to the ultimate goal. This helps us to not only achieve our goals but can also give us lots of small wins and boosts along the way to keep us motivated.
- **Set a date.** Give your goal a date and a time in your busy schedule to achieve what you have set. There is no good in choosing to work out at the gym three times a week and then scheduling no time; you will set yourself up to fail. Choose a time and plan it in. The key to success with goals is giving them time.
- **Don't do too much.** We all have a list of many things we would like to accomplish, but we cannot do them all today. We all want to become more like our Saviour; however, if we wrote the list of what we needed to do for that to happen, we would be overwhelmed. By choosing one focus at a time, we can achieve our goals and even excel in them, and that will motivate us to do more. Failing at goals because we are overwhelmed and overburdened is demotivating.
- **Get a support network!** TEAM. Together everyone achieves more, and as women if we have a great group of friends, our

very own cheerleaders, we will have a better chance of achieving our goals because we will be encouraged and supported along our journey. Never underestimate the power and motivation of a good friend cheering you on, giving you a talking to and redirecting you, or just walking a while by your side to help you achieve your goal. Look for opportunities to be someone else's cheerleader too!

Step Four: Keep It Simple

"But behold I say unto you, that by small and simple things are great things brought to pass." (Alma 37:6)

To enable you to achieve and reach your full potential, keep it simple. Simplify what needs to get done before your day even starts. Being organised enables you to not only free up time each day but simplify the process. One routine that has helped me save time is picking my outfit the night before. This way, I don't feel rushed in the morning, freeing up more time for other things. If your goal is to focus on scripture study, you could put your scriptures out next to your bed and read them in the morning before you check the notifications on your phone.

Living the gospel isn't complicated; growing in spirituality and faith is straightforward and we know where we must start. Begin with the simple things, like talking to Heavenly Father in prayer; this can be a kneeling prayer morning and night or maybe turning off the radio in your car and having a conversation with the Lord as you drive around during the day running errands (this is my personal favourite). He will be your biggest help, so commission Him in your goal setting, asking for His support and guidance.

By your small and simple daily acts, great things do happen. Never underestimate the power of the small and simple things in the world. One drip of water each day will be able to power through even the hardest of rocks.

Step Five: Recharge

We live in a world full of busyness and burnout! Women, wives, and mothers take upon ourselves too much. We struggle not to overload our days physically, mentally, spiritually, and emotionally. We worry too much about those around us in our circle of care and place ourselves at the bottom of the list, if we make the list at all. We take time to plug in our phone every day, forgetting that we, too, need a recharge.

You can achieve great things, but only if you ensure that you are at full charge. How are you expected to make it through each day when you are running on empty? We need to avoid burnout, and to do this we need to make self-love and self-care our top priority. Taking the time to rest and rejuvenate your mind, body, and spirit will help you become re-energised for the next day. Use different strategies that help you relax. Find out what your recharge looks like. It might be meditation, prayer, yoga, a hot bath, a walk, or tucking into a good book. Plan in each day some time for your recharge. This is an excellent help for our mental health and will help reduce stress. Don't feel selfish for taking you time. Feel comforted that because you have, you will be a better friend, wife, sister, and mother. A better woman. It's easy for our minds to wander back to the wiles of busy life, so when you're recharging, focus on recharging!

This recharge should also include charging up our spiritual capacity. The sacrament and our Sabbath day worship account for a part of this, but we need to look for ways to always be filling our oil lamps and being prepared, not just for the bridegroom's coming but for the the everyday events that can chip away at our testimonies and in turn our self-worth and the sacred and essential knowledge of who and whose we are.

Keeping our spiritual, physical, mental, and emotional batteries charged gives us greater ability and strength to cope with all the challenges that each day may bring.

"It all starts by keeping that battery charged along the way—reading the scriptures, saying our prayers, being around good people, and living the gospel."[21]

Here are some quick ideas for self-care and recharge activities that you could do today. Remember, taking care and time for your self is important, and you deserve it!

- Go for a walk—20 mins
- Study a general conference talk—30 mins
- Study *Come, Follow Me*—30 mins
- Listen to a podcast—1 hour
- Curl up with a good book—1 hour
- Journal—15 mins
- Drink a glass of water—8 oz
- Make and enjoy a snack—10 mins

21. Allan F. Packer, "Keep Your Spiritual Batteries Charged," *New Era*, Mar. 2012, 28.

Getting Started: How to Use This Book

There are twenty-five chapters/sections, each focusing on our greatness and the way in which we can develop as women of great faith. They can be read in any order, but we suggest one chapter/section per week. This could be studied together with friends and/or family members who also want to find greater strength and perspective. Many of the chapters have challenges or activities to think about during the week. We suggest that you also think about the goals that we have talked about and maybe, as the weeks pass, mini goals or larger goals will be set or adapted by the things that inspire you. You might also like to journal your progress and the things that you have learned about yourself during that week.

There is also a podcast available on Apple that follows each week of study and introduces many wonderful women of great faith from all over the world. Search the full name of this book on Apple Podcasts to find it.

The biggest thing to remember as you progress through this book is that you are loved, so loved that it is impossible to comprehend. You have a great and glorious work to do here. Embrace the wonderful woman you are.

"The secret of getting ahead is getting started,"[22] so come on—let's go, Girls!

---

22. Author unknown.

1
Your Unique Potential for Greatness

You are unique. Do you really know that? Do you understand and see that uniqueness as beauty and a part of God's incredible design? The world often perceives uniqueness or being different as a negative or demeaning feature. We should, however, look at these individual, unique qualities and individual worth as a glorious gift from our beloved Father in Heaven.

> We are all born with an equal potential for greatness. There are no exceptions, yet most achieve far below their potential while a small handful rise to extraordinary heights and become legends. To rank amongst the elite you must consciously change your habits. Greatness does not show up with time or because you *think* about it. Greatness is a virtue you must consciously invest in every minute of every day. Be intentional about greatness and go after it with an unwavering belief in your abilities to achieve success and excellence.[23]

Today is where we start, right here and right now! This is where we will begin to change, where we will begin to grow to our full potential. When I think of growth and potential, I am reminded of the twenty-year-old wisteria in my garden that has struggled to bloom, like many of us do. I was determined it would reach the measure of its

---

23. Sherrie Campbell, "Develop These 7 Habits to Unlock Your Greatness," Entrepreneur, Dec. 31, 2015.

creation and drape beautiful purple flowers across its foliage, and what a journey it has been! Each summer for eight years, I, along with our gardener, Paul, would study and research all the ways to help it grow but, most of all, the ways to make it flower. Each year after another failure, we set about trying something new. One year it had a massive feed of a special fertiliser or essential nutrient that it may have been lacking, another year we planted a companion plant, the next we loosened the ground around it, one year we gave it more water and then another seriously cut it back. We did so many different things. Each year when the season passed, we had another year of exceptionally healthy, beautiful green foliage—just no flowers. I felt like we had failed again and that maybe we should give up and buy a new plant; maybe we just needed a fresh start. But then I would look at this great plant that had such healthy and beautiful foliage. It didn't flower, but it is still beautiful in its own right, and maybe it was never destined to flower. I could not bring myself to strip it away and start again. So we went back to the books and the drawing board and tried again. Then it happened, in the summer of 2020, a year that we don't like to mention for many reasons but a significant one for my wisteria. I had lost all hope and believed that another year of trying had again been fruitless, but when I spied it, I jumped for joy (and at the time was on a preparation-day call with my missionary son, he wondered why I yelled out with incredible joy); the wisteria had a flower—in fact, in total it had five. They were small and, to the passerby, impossible to see, but I saw them, and it gave me and Paul new hope that we would have success and that this wisteria would be great!

Rolling forward another two years, each year, the wisteria gave us a handful of hidden flowers, as though she was too shy to show her bloom. In the garden, we had the need to remove some very large trees whose roots were coming too close to the house. They were a long distance from the wisteria, but it seemed that their shadows cast over it. That year we didn't do anything to the plant, but it bloomed, covered in beautiful purple foliage. This time I hadn't done anything. What had happened, though, was that the shade had been removed and the plant now had better access to the sun; it was able to bathe in its warmth. It needed full and strong sunlight. Maybe that was what it was missing from its life all along.

The experience of helping my wisteria grow made me think about our Father in Heaven. How often He must look upon us and think we have not met the purpose for which we were planted upon the earth, but like me and my gardener, He doesn't give up. He knows our potential, and He will never stop trying to help us bloom. The experiences of life, the feeds, our companions and friends, and the chopping into the soil and roots where we stand are all part of helping us be strong and reach greatness. This experience also reminded me that the biggest changes in our ability to bloom happen when we bathe in the warmth, in the light and love of the sun, or the Son of God, our Saviour. Having Him in our daily life in a greater way means that we can bloom, and our blossoms will be greater than we could ever imagine.

The wisteria was limited and relied on many external influences beyond its control to reach its potential. We, too, can be influenced by our surroundings and by our connection with the Son along with the good and the bad of daily life; however, we can also help ourselves. We know that we rely wholly upon our Father in Heaven and Saviour for our eternal progression and salvation, but we can still do many things to help us find ways to bloom right here and right now. We can identify through prayer and study our purpose, have integrity, be faithful, daily seek joy and show gratitude, have conviction, make good habits, and remind ourselves constantly of our individual worth. We are not fixed in one place and can move ourselves to be closer to the reach of our Saviour's light.

You really are a great woman. You are the beautiful flower planted here in the garden called Earth; you can bloom right now and change the world around you, bringing joy and hope to your family. The reach of your bloom and light can bring joy in the darkest corners of the world and to those beloved brothers and sisters who are within your reach. You are incredible. Do you appreciate what it means to be you? You are a woman of great faith, you are strong, you have direction, and you know your eternal destination. You are an unstoppable force, a daughter of the King.

The Lord counseled Emma Smith to "lay aside the things of this world, and seek for the things of a better" (Doctrine and Covenants 25:10).

We, too, can take that counsel, but what are those better things? How do you find them and embrace them? For each of us, the answer is as unique and beautiful as we are. Some things we could do are to: strive to be a pioneer, a trendsetter, a game changer, and a spiritual thinker who is deeply driven to make this world a better place. Start within the walls of your own home and become the spiritual anchor your family can depend on. Do not underestimate the power and greatness in this world that you can do within the walls of your own home and the reach of your family. Your home can be a sanctuary from the storms of the world and a place where you can arm your family with faith each day as they battle the storms of life. Let your purpose be doing the Lord's work and loving His people.

"Not everybody can be famous, but everybody can be great because greatness is determined by service."[24]

As we serve within the wall of our own homes, in the community, in our wards, and in our stakes, we will begin to find and embrace our purpose. Find purpose as you minister, as this is part of what Father needs us to do right here and right now. Finding your purpose helps you truly understand the reason for which you were created, the very reason you exist.

> No matter where we live, the makeup of our family, the size of our bank account, or how long we have been a member of the Church, we can each be a powerful influence for good. Living with integrity at home and in the community, using a gentle voice and kind words with a challenging child or difficult coworker, demonstrating your standards by your modest way of dressing, and reaching out of your comfort zone to become acquainted with those who live around you are just some of the many simple actions we can take that will influence others to also rise to a higher plane. (Bingham, "Extraordinary Daughters of God")

Woman of great faith, daughter of the divine. You are here to bloom. This week, take extra time to pay attention to and notice your own personal wisteria plant (metaphorically speaking) and identify

---

24. Attributed to Martin Luther King Jr.

whether you are reaching the measure of your creation. This is where, as women, we become overwhelmed and freak out a little. Just as the wisteria took time to progress, so will you, so work out maybe one or two things that might help you bloom this week or this month. Set a goal and smash it! Imagine the beauty if every sister around the world took a little time this week to help themselves bloom. What a wonderful (or even more wonderful) world we would see.

Remember that there is only one you, and that was the plan! Heavenly Father looked at His incredible creation of the world and His plan of salvation and happiness and realised that for it to be complete, He needed one of you. The exact you that you are! But, more importantly, the incredible YOU that He knew you would become.

- How can I bloom brighter this week?
- What prevents me from blooming?
- How can I change the things that hold me back?

2
Enjoy Each and Every Moment

Life is to be enjoyed and not endured; it isn't about just making it through, but we should be enjoying the journey and the scenery as we take this incredible ride through mortality. Enjoying the moment means that we must have a positive attitude and mindset. What could you change or do today or this week to ensure that you enjoy it and not just endure it?

Very quick, funny story: For the first three years of being a Young Woman I would stand each week and recite the old YW theme. We didn't have it on the wall to read in our ward building, so we just learned it by rote, and I merrily joined in, saying, "We are daughters of our Heavenly Father, who loves us, and we love Him. We will 'stand as witnesses of God at all times and in all things and in all places' as we strive to live the Young Women values, which are: Faith, Divine Nature, Individual Worth, Knowledge, Choice and Accountability, Good Works and Integrity. We believe as we come to accept and act upon these values, we will be prepared to make and keep sacred covenants, receive the ordinances of the temple, and ENDURE the blessings of exaltation." Then the penny dropped—I had been saying it wrong! Just one word I had heard wrong, and then I always repeated it. No one had heard or corrected me, as the difference was so small, seemingly insignificant; however, the whole meaning changed. It should have been ENJOY, not ENDURE, and once I realised my error, I changed it and embraced it with new understanding and hope for this wonderful theme. I now strive every day to ENJOY the blessings of exaltation.

Some days life, family, church responsibilities, community, and daily life can feel like we have to endure rather than enjoy, but making that one change in our outlook and viewpoint can change the whole day, week, and even our entire life.

Enjoying life doesn't mean that it is all rosy and that there are no hard days or heartache; it means that you have an eternal mindset and can see the bigger picture. Even when it comes to the really tough stuff, you can seek out how you can grow from it. This mortal journey has a limited time frame, and therefore, making time to enjoy everything will give us a greater experience.

> Smile. I don't mean that you need to be cracking jokes every day, but a good joke now and then is an escape valve. Life is not all that bad. You will soon learn that everybody has problems and nobody wants to hear about yours. Put those things aside and smile. Have a good sense of humor, as the prophets do. I wish I could tell you some of the things that we talk about.
>
> Not flippant things, not things that are inappropriate—just a good sense of humor. I will tell you a secret of how to wake up in the morning with a smile on your face no matter how you feel: go to bed with a coat hanger in your mouth. Remember, a good sense of humor helps you greatly.[25]

Can we really enjoy each and every moment? If so, how, and what is the secret? How do we get this inner happiness? The obvious answer is living a righteous life, being temple worthy, and having a positive outlook. It requires a glass-half-full and not half-empty attitude, seeing the silver linings in the clouds and striving to find the good in the middle of every storm. So what can you do to increase the joy in your life and on your journey today, this week, this year?

I had a little joy project as a teenager, which embarrassed my mum and my siblings, but I got a huge kick out of it! To give you some context, in our home the back of the bathroom door was covered in quotes and uplifting thoughts. My mum had figured that she had a captive audience, and it worked. Those quotes are ingrained in my mind. But one that I loved and tested out was "If you see someone

---

25. Richard G. Scott, "Living a Life of Peace, Joy, and Purpose," *Ensign* or *Liahona*, Feb. 2014, 19–20.

without a smile, give them one of yours."[26] And next to it was one that said "Smile. It's contagious."

So I decided that I was going to do just that. I was about thirteen years old, and when we went anywhere, I would intentionally gain eye contact with people who were not smiling and give them a big smile, often accompanied by a Hello. It perplexed people; they would look around to work out whether I was smiling or talking to them, and then it would happen—that magical moment when they "caught it," they would smile back. It was almost like a little competition I had with myself to see how many people I could make smile. It was great fun and thoroughly embarrassing for those people who were with me. I highly recommend it.

Our wonderful modern-day prophets have given us ideas and insights into how we might increase the joy in our lives.

President Gordon B. Hinckley taught that the more often a person says thank you, the happier he will be. "There are two little words in the English language that mean more than all others," he said. "They are 'thank you.'"[27]

This is one of the very first things we are taught, to say the "magic words" of please and thank you, but as adults, without the right attitude, it could be easy to get stuck in the wrong mindset and use the magic words less and less. Why not take part in a little experiment this week? Keep track of how many times you say thank you in a typical day, and evaluate whether there were more times you could have said it and didn't. Then make an effort to increase that number. Saying thank you helps us enjoy the moments and develops an attitude of gratitude.

"Years ago President David O. McKay gave this valuable counsel to Latter-day Saints: 'Start out to make somebody else happy and see how quickly your own soul is filled with joy.'"[28]

---

26. Attributed to Dolly Parton.
27. Gordon B. Hinckley, "A Prophet's Counsel and Prayer for Youth," *Ensign*, Jan. 2001, from youth and young adult fireside Nov. 12, 2000.
28. Larry R. Lawrence, "Choose Happiness," Brigham Young University devotional, Mar. 8, 2016, speeches.byu.edu.

With so much going on, it's easy to just go, go, go and not take the time to smell the flowers. Enjoy the moments that you experience throughout each day. This will help you feel grateful and appreciative of what you have in your life. Enjoy the simple things, like having a roof over your head and being able to afford food for your family. Have you ever taken a walk with a toddler? That is one way to find real joy. Look at the world through their eyes, and it is INCREDIBLE. Each leaf, flower, worm, pebble, and crack in the pavement is something amazing that needs to be explored, enjoyed, and possibly stuffed into a chubby little hand or pocket to be enjoyed again later.

We don't have time to live and love everything the way a toddler does; however, we can learn from them as we are taught to "become as little children" (Matthew 18:3; see also verse 4), simplify what we see in joy and happiness, break it into little pieces that we can collect in our metaphorical pockets, savor them, and enjoy them again and again.

Although being productive is important, taking the time to enjoy each moment is important too. I have a wonderful sign in my kitchen that is a daily reminder. It says, "Happiness is an inside job," and that is true. Only we can choose to be happy even in the hard times, only we can choose to find the silver linings in the storm, and only we can find the million little moments of potential joy in each and every day.

This week as you strive to find more joy, why not make a joy list or a happy list? You can use a phone or a notepad and write down every little thing that brings you joy. This may end up being a HUGE list, so be prepared! You might include simple things like a text or a message you get from a friend, a phone call, the sun shining, birdsong, clean clothes drying on the line, a chocolate bar, a moment with your child, a talk or lesson at church, a smile from a stranger, not tripping over the children's shoes at the back door, or someone emptying the dishwasher! This list will grow, and you will see how many wonderful moments you can enjoy. Reread them and take an extra moment to really appreciate them. To help you extend this joy, share it with those you love—they might not realise how happy or joyful it made them when they did a simple act of service or just gave you a hug goodnight. This list might also help you identify the ways you can help bring joy to others.

You are a woman of great faith who can find, embrace, and share joy with those you meet each day; you can fill your cup of joy as you identify the many joyous experiences you have each day.

Remember always what President Nelson has taught: "The joy we feel has little to do with the circumstances of our lives and everything do to with the focus of our lives."[29]

---

29. Russell M. Nelson, "Joy and Spiritual Survival," *Ensign* or *Liahona*, Nov. 2016, 82.

3
Always Improving

"President Spencer W. Kimball (1895–1985) continually encouraged us to 'lengthen our stride' and to 'enlarge our vision.'"[30]

You are here and you are in the third week, so therefore you are striving to be always improving. Well done. Keep it up—you've got this! You are a woman of great faith, and you are growing each and every day towards your true potential.

Life is like learning to play an instrument, I am going to select the piano, as this is one instrument I have taken lessons on my whole life to learn to play a little, and without any greatness. But I have learned, and I always try to be a little better than I was before. It doesn't happen by accident or just by having a piano in my home; it doesn't happen by buying a new music book or by hoping and longing. Only by taking time, effort, and continued practice can I improve. It will take a whole lifetime, or maybe even an eternity, for me to be a great pianist, but I know that I can one day get there if I just do my part. This analogy can be related to each and every one of us. We are all here, better than we once were, and have learned so much already, but we are still just fumbling over the keys and just about making out a tune in the song of eternity. So we need to keep it up, we need to practice,

30. Donald L. Staheli, "Achieving Your Full Potential," *Ensign* or *Liahona*, Feb. 2009, 57.

we need to try each day, and most importantly, we need to try again when it just doesn't sound right or we forget the notes.

In the last session of each general conference, our beloved prophet speaks to us, and he will often remind us to strive to be better. Each message is different, but the overall thought is to be a little better over the next six months before the next conference than we have been in the past. Take a look at these beautiful messages over the last few conferences and see how he is asking us to better ourselves. These messages come from our Father in Heaven and Saviour via our prophet, and we need to heed these words. In the October 2021 conference, President Russell M. Nelson said, "I plead with you today to counter the lure of the world by making time for the Lord in your life—each and every day."[31]

Being a little better, making time for the Lord each and every day for six months is an incredible goal and one we can ALL achieve, one that will help each of us improve. We decide how much a little is—and I want you to really take a moment to think about it. Don't set yourself up to fail here. What is a little? If this were a physical workout to increase the distance you ran, we wouldn't ever say, "I can just about do a mile, so I want to run a marathon each day." We would probably say, "Okay, let's get the mile under our belt and done and try another half a mile." Our Father in Heaven wants us to learn, but He reminds us always that we need to do it at a realistic pace. Isaiah 28:10 says, "For precept must be upon precept, precept upon precept; line upon line, line upon line; here a little, and there a little." Each time we do a little better and achieve a little more, it is like we've added a small building block in our great faith; it takes time, and that is okay. Some days will be roaring successes, and some days we will feel like we are flat on our faces in a muddy puddle. But, thankfully, your speed doesn't matter. Forward is still forward.

Using our new mindset of joy from last week and understanding the processes we need to take to bloom, let's celebrate our successes and the progress we've made. Let's not beat ourselves up or give up when things don't go to plan or how we might have hoped. Slow and steady wins the race, and you have to remember that your only

---

31. Russell M. Nelson, "Make Time for the Lord," *Liahona*, Nov. 2021, 120.

competition in the race is you! Don't compare, as your improvement can only ever be marked against you. So be your own cheerleader and get your friends and family to also cheer you on (cheerleaders are a huge help along our mortal journey; mine are precious to me and have helped me more than they will ever be able to understand). Mark your progress and set the next mini goal; this won't be a today, this week, or even this month goal; it is an always goal. Maybe you could set a goal in an area of your life that you could work on for the next conference, and then each conference do the same, using each as a benchmark. We can also use conference as an inspiration for areas of our life that need improvement.

We have been taught, "Always be improving yourself. Set personal achievement goals and stretch to accomplish them. Improve yourself physically, socially, mentally, and spiritually . . . Keep growing and learning and progressing and serving others."[32]

We improve and grow in so many areas in our lives and often don't realise the progress that we have made until we look back; just as we might measure a child with marks on a wall to see their growth, we should be marking our current place and then measuring our progress. Doing this will spur us on to do more, to be better, to improve in even greater ways. Our personal progress is measured in the Children and Youth program, but we can in our journals do the very same thing now. Set a small goal, and use the steps we covered earlier in the book to make it a success.

Let's specifically set goals based on the message from our beloved prophet to make time for the Lord each and every day. What does that look like? What do you do already in your day to make time for Him? I suspect that we will all be able to find areas in which to improve in this challenge. President Nelson went on to make some suggestions, and these might help you as you make your plan.

> My brothers and sisters, I plead with you to. . . . Make your own spiritual foundation firm and able to stand the test of time by doing those things that allow the Holy Ghost to be with you *always*. . . .

---

32. Ezra Taft Benson, "To the Single Adult Sisters of the Church," *Ensign*, Nov. 1988, 97.

> Nothing invites the Spirit more than fixing your focus on Jesus Christ.
>
> Talk of Christ, rejoice in Christ, feast upon the words of Christ, and press forward with steadfastness in Christ. Make your Sabbath a delight as you worship Him, partake of the sacrament, and keep His day holy.
>
> As I emphasized this morning, please make time for the Lord in His holy house. Nothing will strengthen your spiritual foundation like temple service. . . .
>
> The Lord knows you and loves you. He is your Savior and your Redeemer. He leads and guides His Church. He will lead and guide *you* in your personal life.[33]

In her book *Covenant Keepers*, Sister Nelson shared an experience where she switched listening to the local radio in her car each morning to listen to the scriptures, and this had a profound impact on her day; this simple change could help you as it helped Sister Nelson. Have a conversation with the Lord as you drive in the car or as you do your shopping, and listen to the scriptures as you go about your day. Giving time for the scriptures daily has NEVER been easier than it is now; we have them on our phones and have an endless resource of inspiration at our fingertips. Next time you are at the doctor's office, instead of reading a magazine or playing a game on your phone or surfing the web, why not read the scriptures or the *Come, Follow Me* lesson? Small changes will lead to big improvements.

You are a woman of great faith, and as your greatness grows, so must your relationship with Father and our Saviour Jesus Christ. They are there ALWAYS, and They want to help you become even greater. The Saviour will lead and guide you; as you let Him, He will prompt and inspire you. Take some quiet time today and this week to really be with Him.

---

33. Russell M. Nelson, "Make Time for the Lord," *Liahona*, Nov. 2021, 120–21.

"We, your brethren, need your strength, your conversion, your conviction, your ability to lead, your wisdom, and your voices. The kingdom of God is not and cannot be complete without women who make sacred covenants and then keep them, women who can speak with the power and authority of God!"[34]

34. Russell M. Nelson, "A Plea to My Sisters," *Ensign* or *Liahona*, Nov. 2015, 96.

4
He Loves Us Too Much

"The Lord loves each of us too much to merely let us go on being what we now are, for he knows what we have the possibility to become!"[35]

Each and every one of us is blessed with the most loving Father in Heaven and the most incredible big brother in Jesus Christ. These two along with Heavenly Mother and the Holy Spirit love us fiercely. They send each one of us to Earth from their loving, heavenly embrace on to our mortal mission, with great joy at the fabulous opportunities before us; however, having had a son on his mission, I know from personal experience how much parents worry about their precious children, and I am sure that our heavenly family feels the same way. They look forward to hearing from us through prayer, just as I looked forward to my preparation-day calls. They will want to help us have the best mortal mission and that we can grow from every moment of it. Father didn't just send us and leave us to it; He loves us too much for that. He will do all He can to provide opportunities and people to help us along our journey, to lift us, and to love us.

Just as a child might be encouraged to do a hard thing to grow and learn or to step outside their comfort zone, Father asks this of us too. Parents encourage children to grow and take the next step

35. Neal A. Maxwell, "In Him All Things Hold Together," Brigham Young University devotional, Mar. 31, 1991, speeches.byu.edu.

towards greatness, and they stand beside their children, ready to offer love and support in just the same way our Heavenly Parents do with us. What is Father encouraging you to do right now? What is your next step? These are questions only YOU know the answer to, but understanding what is next and knowing He is there to love and support you should give you strength.

"When we understand who God is, who we are, how He loves us, and what His plan is for us, fear evaporates."[36]

Fear holds us back, trips us up, and prevents our progression, but what do we fear? If we fail, we are just learning new ways of how not to do something. Thomas Edison, rather than being focused on his failed attempts, once said, "I have gotten a lot of results! I know several thousand things that won't work."[37] If he had given up at any one of those failures, he would not have known the great and wonderful joy of success.

"God's plan of happiness is all about you. You are His precious child and of great worth. He knows and loves you."[38]

This is it; it is simple, and it is true. YOU are His. YOU matter to Him. YOU are part of His work and His glory. YOU are so important to Him that you can never be forgotten or overlooked.

"For God so loved [YOU], that he gave His only begotten Son, that [as YOU believe] in him [YOU] should not perish, but have everlasting life." (John 3:16)

This great plan, the one in which a Saviour was sent to Earth, was made because HE loves YOU. The most incredible events in the history of the world were all put in place because He loves YOU. That precious babe in a manger was here for YOU, that great man

---

36. John H. Groberg, "The Power of God's Love," *Ensign* or *Liahona*, Nov. 2004, 10.

37. Frank Lewis Dyer and Thomas Commerford Martin, *Edison: His Life and Inventions*, volume 2, (New York: Harper & Brothers, New York, 1910), 616.

38. Alan T. Phillips, "God Knows and Loves You," *Liahona*, Nov. 2023, 51.

performing miracles lived for YOU, and that loving brother pled with the Father to take upon Himself YOUR sins. Don't ever think that you are overlooked, unwanted, insignificant. You are not. The God and Creator of this wonderful world knows you, loves you, and has created a plan for YOU to be able to achieve greatness. It is packed with do-overs and second chances because He loves you enough to be there to help you overcome the hard stuff, and he loves you regardless of what has transpired.

> So many have been hurt by broken and strained relationships that it is difficult for them to believe in God's compassion and long-suffering. They struggle to see God as He is—a loving Father who meets us in our need and knows how to "give good things to them that ask him." His grace is not just a prize for the worthy. It is the "divine assistance" He gives that helps us become worthy. It is not just a reward for the righteous. It is the "endowment of strength" He gives that helps us become righteous. We are not just walking *toward* God and Christ. We are walking *with* Them.[39]

His love is abundant in the beautiful gift of forgiveness. I like to imagine that just as I would hold close a child when they have come to apologise for a transgression and would assure them that it is okay, that the transgression can be forgotten now but help them change and talk through some ideas of how to prevent it from happening again; that this is how Father is with us. As we take our broken hearts to Him and plead for forgiveness, He puts his loving arms around us, letting us know it will be okay. He assures us that His love is constant and that He believes in us and that we are forgiven, but He also wants us to take the time to evaluate how we got to where we are and plan how can it be avoided in the future. I also know that He will be there when I inevitably stumble and fall in the future.

His great love for YOU is there as you take the sacrament each week. As you have the chance to clean the slate with Him and start anew, remember the covenants you have made, and set the compass right for the next week of your mortal adventure.

I invite you this week to take time to look for the beautiful love notes that Father in Heaven leaves for you, those notes of encouragement

39. Bradley R. Wilcox, "Worthiness Is Not Flawlessness,", *Liahona*, Nov. 2021, 67.

and direction, that remind you that you are loved, that you have got this, or that you are enough. I find that the beautiful primary song "My Heavenly Father Loves Me"[40] helps me see these metaphorical love notes abundantly everywhere (feel free to sing it this week), and when we feel loved, we thrive, we grow, and we find the strength and hope that enables us to move forward through the day.

What are the beautiful things in nature or the world around you that help you appreciate and see God's hand and His love notes just for you? In England there is a place called the North Yorkshire Moors that is so barren and often described as bleak, but I find the grandeur of it exquisite—the outstanding beauty when it turns varied shades of purple in August and September as the heather blooms and the rolling hills turn into a sea of purple. There have been many places as I have travelled the world that take my breath away as to the beauty of Heavenly Father's creations and the world He made for me to enjoy.

This week talk to Father, evaluate where you're at and which way you can grow, embrace the beautiful gift of the Atonement, and keep a record of His love notes to you. Remember, woman of great faith, that YOU are His, YOU are Loved, and in Father, you have the greatest life coach, companion, and cheerleader. YOU can do this!

"Be strong and of good courage. You are truly royal spirit daughters of Almighty God. You are princesses, destined to become queens. Your own wondrous story has already begun. Your 'once upon a time' is now."[41]

---

40. *Children's Songbook*, 228.

41. Dieter F. Uchtdorf, "Your Happily Ever After," *Ensign* or *Liahona*, May 2010, 127.

5
Take Responsibility

We are all on the most amazing mortal journey, but we must always remember that we control the path we take, we are the authors of our own destiny, and the past chapters of our lives have no control over where we choose to steer ourselves in the future.

There is a saying that "Yesterday is history, tomorrow is a mystery, today is a gift of God, which is why we call it the present" (attributed to Bill Keane). this is almost correct; however, tomorrow is not a total mystery. It is our choice. We can be what we want to be and go where we want to go, and it's never too late to spread our wings and fly with new dreams and ideas in mind.

We talk a lot about our life being a journey, and it is, but we often forget that we planned this trip way back in the premortal realm; we chose many of the adventures and experiences that we have. The good, the bad, and the indifferent are all aspects of this mortal experience, and we came to Earth to feel all these feelings and to understand more about Father. In our hardest moments, when we feel like we cannot make it, we need to remember that this is what we wanted; we wanted to experience mortality as a part of the plan of salvation and happiness. We need to take each day, regardless of how hard it is, and ask ourselves how what happens today can help us be more like our Heavenly Father and Heavenly Mother.

> "Is the road you are now traveling and the present conduct of your life leading you to achieve your full God-given potential? If you were to make no changes in the present course of your life, would you be happy with who you are and what you have become five years from now?"[42]

That being said, we don't just amble along and hope for the best! We write our own stories and choose our destiny. This was another part of the plan—that we would be able to have choices about how we would live our life and what we would like to achieve.

> "How lucky are you that you are alive today? Don't forget to live. Choose to live beautifully; it will define your destiny."[43]

There are some key things we need to consider that will help us take responsibility for our life, our destiny, and who we will become.

Be accountable. It sounds simple, but this is one thing that we often let slide. It can be far too hard to actually acknowledge that maybe we influenced the things that are hard or are happening to us. If we are accountable, we take control; this is the first step to master our own destiny.

To be accountable, we need to stop blaming others. We cannot point fingers at another person's actions and behaviour and give them power over our life. It's YOUR life, and YOU are sailing your ship!

On your metaphorical ship, you cannot control the weather. You can control when you sail and take advice on things that might impact your journey, but you cannot stop a storm or a surge. When we experience a stormy day or when our days seem clouded, we need to acknowledge what happened and not avoid it or hide from it. Reset your compass and don't give up.

> "Every day may not be good . . . but there's something good in every day."[44]

42. Staheli, "Achieving Your Potential," 57–8.

43. Attributed to Debasish Mridha.

44. Attributed to Alice Morse Earle.

Be positive, move through your day with a positive attitude, and make sure your glass is always half full. Don't allow the negative and cynical underlying emotions to surface; you are bigger and better than that. However, if it rears its ugly head, then just reset and find your half-full glass. There are hard and sad emotions that we all feel, they have their place and time but when we take time to reset and focus on the positive our mindset and day can be better,

---

"Your future happiness, personal righteousness, and relationship with the Lord will depend in large part on the habits you embrace and the choices and commitments you make over the next few years."[45]

Take some time for yourself this week to look at the plan of your current journey and destination. What is your biggest dream? Who do you really want to be? What is stopping you? NO dream is too big or impossible. YOU have all the skills, abilities, and resources for greatness deep within you. Father sent you here to Earth with the ability. You just need to unlock, practice, and perfect the belief that YOU can do this, YOU have got it, and YOU deserve it! Have the courage to be different from those in the world around you. Don't ever forget YOU are a beautiful, heavenly being having a mortal experience.

Just remember these four tools in your armoury that will help you and remember that the Lord will bless you and strengthen you so that you may magnify yourself and embrace the incredible future YOU have:

1. Be continually developing your testimony. Treat it like a muscle that you can strengthen as a woman of great faith.

President Russell M. Nelson taught us: "Attacks against the Church, its doctrine, and our way of life are going to increase. Because of this, we need women who have a bedrock understanding of the doctrine of Christ and who will use that understanding to teach and help raise a sin-resistant generation. We need women who can detect deception in all of its forms. We need women who know how to access

45. Staheli, "Achieving Your Potential," 57.

the power that God makes available to covenant keepers and who express their beliefs with confidence and charity. We need women who have the courage and vision of our Mother Eve."[46]

2. Developing our testimony helps our faith grow. The little seedling of faith within us can grow into a mighty oak. You are a woman of great faith, so much greater than you could ever imagine.

Elder M. Russell Ballard has said:

> Nothing is more remarkable or important in this life than to know that God our Eternal Father and his Son, Jesus Christ, have spoken again from the heavens and have called prophets and apostles to teach the fullness of the everlasting gospel once again upon the earth. That is a glorious thing to know. When you know it, that knowledge affects your life. It influences every major decision you make. It changes the course of your life to a safer one because it provides an anchor that helps hold you fast to the teachings of the gospel despite the evil influences all around you that entice you to drift toward sin and transgression.[47]

3. Pray daily, pray often, and pray always. Have your heart and mind open to a conversation with the Lord at all times and in all places. YOU are a woman of great faith who leans upon Father through prayer.

A woman of faith trusts God and faces adversity with hope. She knows of His interest in her life. She knows that He knows her. She loves His words and drinks deeply of that living water. She is grateful for the prophet He has sent for these latter days, and she trusts his counsel and follows it, for she knows that by so doing she will find safety and peace.

In prayer she seeks the kind, unfaltering guidance and help of a listening Heavenly Father. As she prays, she listens—allowing the communication to be two-way. She trusts that in His still and

---

46. Russell M. Nelson, "A Plea to My Sisters," 97.

47. M. Russell Ballard, "Anchor to the Soul," Brigham Young University devotional, Sept. 6, 1992, speeches.byu.edu.

quiet way, He will lead her by the hand and give her answer to her prayers.[48]

4. Don't just read the words that have been preserved in the holy scriptures; study them, devour them, and digest them. As a woman of great faith, let the scriptures become a part of you.

> When I study the scriptures, the Spirit of the Lord fills my home. I gain important understanding, which I then share with my family, and my love for them increases. The Lord has told us that our time should "be devoted to the studying of the scriptures" (D&C 26:1) and that "the Book of Mormon and the holy scriptures are given ... for [our] instruction" (D&C 33:16). Every woman can be a gospel doctrine instructor in her home, and every sister in the Church needs gospel knowledge as a leader and teacher. If you have not already developed the habit of daily scripture study, start now and keep studying in order to be prepared for your responsibilities in this life and in the eternities. (Julie B. Beck, "My Soul Delighteth in the Scriptures," *Ensign* or *Liahona*, May 2004, 107–8)

You, as a woman of GREAT faith, trust in YOUR loving Father in Heaven, you know that your older brother Jesus Christ has your back, you know that They have an interest in YOUR daily life, you know that They know you, you love the words of the Saviour, and you will drink deeply of His living water, HIS words, and His Love.

48. Margaret D. Nadauld, "A Woman of Faith," *Ensign* or *Liahona*, Nov. 2002.

6
Your Talents

The Savior's parable of the talents is so applicable to you at this stage in your life. He knows there are differences between each of you intellectually, emotionally, and physically. The Lord only expects you to magnify and develop the talents and abilities you have been given. But He also expects you to be accountable for your actions in so doing. Take control of your actions and prepare to succeed at whatever you are capable of doing.[49]

This is an area that is a HUGE problem for many of us. We don't identify our incredible God-given talents but instead compare ourselves to others and try to benchmark ourselves against other women. THIS HAS TO STOP right now! Although it is good to be inspired by others, you have to remember that there is ONE you. "Be yourself; everyone else is already taken."[50] You were sent to this earth to be unique, not a copy and paste. You have exceptional skills and talents. Some of them you will have already developed, whereas some are waiting in the wings for the future.

So what are your talents? Or, more importantly, what are talents? The *Oxford English Dictionary* tells us that a talent is "[someone who has] a natural ability to be good at something, especially without being taught." This might be true, but I have always found developing

49. Staheli, "Achieving Your Potential," 58.

50. Attributed to Oscar Wilde.

a talent to be hard work, difficult to achieve, and an uphill struggle. Our talents and abilities are gifts from our Heavenly Father; every person is endowed with many because He loves us so much. Write a list right now to identify what talents you have, which you know need work, and your ultimate talent bucket list—the ones you want to develop.

If you are struggling to work out your incredible and lengthy list of talents, here are some things we can do to help identify them:

Pray. Prayer is ALWAYS a great starting point; Heavenly Father knows us and knows us eternally. He knows what talents we had in the premortal existence and knows the ones that we have yet to discover. He knows what we can achieve. We have to search and discover our talents and then work on them.

Ask for a priesthood/father's blessing to help recognise and identify your unique talents, those that you already have, and what you need to seek to develop so that you can bless your life and the lives of your family, friends, wards, and community. We should receive and study our patriarchal blessing (photocopy it and write notes, highlight areas, journal on it, doodle if you need, or whatever helps you to study and understand it more). It will be scattered with details of talents we either have or need to develop. We could also speak to those we love and ask them what they think our talents are. You will be surprised by what others see in you that you may have overlooked. This can also be a great home evening activity.

Writing these down in a list can be empowering as we see these things in black and white, but also potentially a little overwhelming. Just as with most things in life, we can start small, so some of our talents might right now be a little seed a long way from the flower it can become, but it requires a process to get there, just as taking that seedling, planting it, and nourishing it to full bloom. Some progress might require training or formal education or require us to overcome special challenges. When we identify, develop, or define our talents, it can often be a domino effect, and we discover new skills and attributes.

You might be thinking that this chapter is not for you. Don't think that you are just ordinary and you are not actually that talented. That IS NOT true. You learned many amazing things before you even came to this earth, and those talents transferred to mortality. You may not be musical or artistic, you might not be a wiz in the kitchen or great at home décor; however, these are just a few of the millions, actually billions, of talents that Father may have taught and shared with His children.

"Human tragedies: We all want to be extraordinary and we all just want to fit in. Unfortunately, extraordinary people rarely fit in."[51]

The reality is YOU ARE extraordinary. Don't allow yourself to be anything else. You don't want to fit in; you were designed to stand out and be admired. Your talents could include kindness, friendship, the ability to listen, empathy, compassion, teaching, leading, peacemaking, prayerfulness, understanding the scriptures . . . the list continues, but find your talents and excel at them.

One at a time, take your talents and do your absolute best with them. The Apostle Paul said, "Neglect not the gift that is in thee" (1 Timothy 4:14). But finding and improving your talents will require effort. Do not all of a sudden feel overwhelmed and as if it is just too much. You do have many, many talents, but just as my wonderful stake president (Sean Roberts) once said, "If I asked you to eat an elephant, you would say it was just too much; however, you can eat the elephant. You just have to do it one mouthful at a time." Taking this approach means that we can go about our progress one bite at a time, always moving forward but with a realistic plan. Some talents will be developed naturally and with minimal effort, but you should evaluate yourself and your progress against the most important person: YOU. Ask yourself, *Am I better today than I was yesterday? Have I progressed since last week, month, or year?* "Just do the best you can, but be sure it is your very best!"[52]

We need to celebrate our talents, too, and not be embarrassed by what we have achieved. We don't need to brag or show off, but rather share, share, share. One of the purposes of talents is the joy of helping,

---

51. Attributed to Sebastyne Young.

52. Gordon B. Hinckley, "A Challenging Time—a Wonderful Time," An Evening with President Gordon B. Hinckley, Feb. 7, 2003, 5.

lifting, encouraging, and developing our brothers and sisters on this mortal journey with us. One of the most beautiful talents we can have is to love, develop, and teach others.

One more thing that we need to remember is that just as we learned skills and gained talents in the premortal realms and mortality, our talents, skills, and attributes are eternal. The things that we are working on now and trying to develop and be better at might never be perfected during our mortality, but that should never stop us. One day in the eternities, I hope to be able to play the piano well enough that I could pick up any piece of music, play it, and enjoy it. I am glad that I will have mortality, the millennium, and eternity to perfect this. Knowing that I have all this time to become better takes the pressure off, but it shouldn't create a complacent attitude. What talents do you have that you know will take time to perfect? Sometimes these are not yet talents but goals, desires, or ambitions. Examine your interests, seek a new talent, then develop it.

President Boyd K. Packer said, "Go to, then, you who are gifted; cultivate your gift. Develop it in any of the arts and in every worthy example of them. If you have the ability and the desire, seek a career or employ your talent as an avocation or cultivate it as a hobby. But in all ways bless others with it. Set a standard of excellence. . . . Never express your gift unworthily."[53]

Author Erma Bombeck is attributed to have said, "When I stand before God at the end of my life, I would hope that I would not have a single bit of talent left, and could say, 'I used everything you gave me.'"

As a woman of great faith, we need to be more like Erma. We need to remember that developing these gifts and talents given to us by Father shows us how we love Him. It represents and indicates our desire to learn and be better, and it fulfills our desire as spirit children who wanted to come to Earth and become more like Father. YOU have so many talents within you. Write the list, make a plan, choose which bite of this elephant of eternal talents you are going to take this week, and do it! Often, developing a talent can be enjoyable and actually look more like you time, and that is okay. That was part of

53. The Arts and the Spirit of the Lord, in *Speeches of the Year, 1976* [1977], 280.

Father's plan, too, for us to have time for ourselves. It is not selfish; it is essential for our progression. However, there are also times and seasons in our life where we have more time, capacity, money, or energy to work on certain talents and skills, so always be realistic and establish where you are right now and what YOU need. Allow yourself to be WOW (a woman of worth).

7
Stay Focused and Use Your Time Wisely

"Time is the most valuable thing a [woman] can spend."[54]

We all came to Earth for our mortal experience. Our time would be filled with incredible and terrifying experiences, a total roller coaster of events that would help us become more like Father. Every moment is a gift.

We need to cherish our time and use it wisely. In the UK, between 2009 and 2016, we spent hours each day on the mundane and functional; we slept for an average of eight and a half hours per day (although, it might often have felt like less with small children or teenagers in seminary!), an average of one and a half hours per day was spent in unpaid/voluntary work, almost two and a half hours per day watching TV, and approximately an hour and twenty minutes eating meals (see ourworldindata.org/time-use). Many of these things are requirements, but we still have hours left to focus and prioritise the really important stuff. How much time each day do we spend in prayer, studying the scriptures, and studying our *Come, Follow Me* lessons? How much time have you spent on your talents? Time with your family? Serving your family, ward, community, or those you are assigned to be a minister to?

54. Attributed to Theophrastus.

"Our family is the focus of our greatest work and joy in this life; so will it be throughout all eternity."[55]

Part of the process of using our time wisely is planning and establishing how we use our time and evaluating whether we are using it as we should or as we would like to. Spend a few minutes each day or each week to make a plan for how you can best use your time to become the BEST and to be the GREATEST version of yourself. "The key is in not 'spending' time, but in 'investing' it."[56] We need to invest in ourselves, so always build a little into your schedule for YOU. Does this time include a bubble bath or an extra-long shower, a walk with the dog, or a few minutes cuddled up in your chair reading a book or just watching the birds out of the window? Give yourself permission to factor in YOU time.

"There's only one thing more precious than our time, and that's who we spend it on" (attributed to Leo Christopher). Who in your life do you want to give your time to? Do you spend it on your colleagues at work, friends, or your family? Do you give your family an even share of quality time? Do you give your Saviour or Father in Heaven enough time in your day?

The most significant part of managing your time wisely is to know what your focus is. What is the prize that your eyes are on? Is it the goal of eternity and life in the celestial kingdom with all your family? Is it getting a handle on the work-life balance in your life? Being focused and achieving well-spent time is to stay on course, on the road, on the straight and narrow. It is to take one step in front of the other, closer and closer to your destination. Never underestimate the progress you have already made along the road.

> I am convinced that distractions and discouragement are some of Satan's most effective tools. He finds ways to help us make excuses about why we can't do this or that. He gets us involved in wasting our time and resources in things that lead us away from improving

55. Russell M. Nelson, "Set in Order Thy House," *Ensign*, Nov. 2001, 71.

56. Stephen R. Covey, *First Things First Every Day* (Simon & Schuster, 1997), 128.

> our lives and developing our talents. He blurs our focus by diverting our attention. This can happen to the very best of you.[57]

Therefore, being focused involves us controlling and managing the distractions of the world, not letting Satan wedge his foot into the door of our day, not even for a moment. We should take the warnings in the Book of Mormon seriously; we need to remember that these passages of scripture were written for us, every one of us. YOU, as a woman of great faith, it was written for you, as Father knew that Satan would want you, your time, and your efforts wasted on him and his plans.

"And others will he pacify, and lull them away into carnal security, that they will say: All is well in Zion; yea, Zion prospereth, all is well—and thus the devil cheateth their souls, and leadeth them away carefully down to hell." (2 Nephi 28:21). I spent a lot of time talking with my Dad about this scripture, and we liked to make it personal, which really helped me focus on what was important. We are taught to relate the scriptures to ourselves.

I would tell myself: Satan will pacify, calm, placate, and appease me with worldly security; he will make me think that all is well in my home, my calling, my ministering, and my family, let me think that I am doing a good job (so I become prideful) in what I do in the gospel, and that's it! He has got me. He can lead me carefully down to hell!

This scripture was preserved for active, busy members of the Church, ones who read and study the scriptures, ones who would see this and be in a position to make the necessary changes. This is one of those notes Father has left for us to prevent us from heartache and loss and to enable us to stay close to Him. It was written for YOU as a woman of great faith.

I need to remember that I cannot take my eye off the ball (not even for a second) of eternal progression and development for myself or my family; we should never coast or think we have got it. That is when Satan can get a grip on us.

This week take a check of yourself against this scripture. Are you coasting, or are you rowing against the currents of the world? What are you being pacified by? What is your carnal or worldly security

57. Staheli, "Achieving Your Potential," 58.

blanket? What is the warning that YOU need to hear from this message from Father? What is He telling YOU?

Only we can choose what our focus is or should be; only you can decide what or who to spend your time on, and only YOU can choose to coast or to row. However, we have been given some guidance on how we might like to spend time or how we might need to.

"If you want to change the world go home and love your family."[58]

"No other success in life can compensate for failure in the home."[59]

"The greatest work you will ever do will be within the walls of your own home."[60]

Home should be the focus; it should be where much of our time and efforts are, regardless of what our family unit might look like. This does not mean that we all need to be stay-at-home mums—many of us don't have that luxury—however, a working mum widow, daughter, sister, wife, or aunt can still very firmly have her focus on her home, and "Homes filled with love are a joy, a delight, a literal heaven on earth."[61] And as the beautiful hymn teaches us, they can be a place of safety, a haven in the world, a place of learning, and a place where we are taught to connect with our Father in Heaven (see "Home Can Be a Heaven on Earth," *Hymns*, no. 298). Homes that are heavenly in the way they love, accept, and include family members become places that are sacred, as we all need a place to belong and a place of sanctuary. Every moment spent in our homes and building our families' earthly havens is priceless.

---

58. Attributed to Mother Theresa.

59. David O. McKay quoting J. E. McCulloch, *Home: The Savior of Civilization* (1924), 42; in Conference Report, Apr. 1935, 116.

60. Harold B. Lee, "Maintain Your Place as a Woman," *Ensign*, Feb. 1972, 51.

61. Quentin L. Cook, "Great Love for Our Father's Children," *Ensign*, May 2019, 79.

"Staying focused, disciplined, and committed to meaningful goals, both spiritual and temporal, is an important—in fact, an essential—key to your success here in this life and in the eternities to come."[62]

Your future happiness, your personal righteousness, and your precious relationship with YOUR Father is dependent upon the way you spend your time, the focus of your behaviour, and the habits and choices that you embrace—the commitments and covenants that YOU make.

You are a woman of great faith who listens to Father and heeds the warnings He has given. Your great faith is what drives you; it leads you and enables you to row against the tides and push against the storms. You can constantly readjust yourself each day, and you CAN stay focused. You can identify the important and choose NOT TO coast. You can choose YOUR direction.

62. Staheli, "Achieving Your Potential," 59.

8
Have the Courage to Be Different

We have all played the game of dares as a child. I am inviting you to play it again now, but this time it is serious. I dare you to be different. I dare you to be unique. I dare you to stand tall and firm in your beliefs. I dare you to be a woman of great faith who never wavers.

When you were young, you were uninhibited by what others thought of you, whether your clothes or shoes matched, or whether the makeup you attempted to apply seemed to be inspired by a clown rather than your mum! You would strut out with a wiggle in your step, elated with your success. Why did you stop? What took away your confidence to wear what you liked and be who you wanted to be, one of a kind?

Growing older makes us more aware of ourselves, and we begin to conform to social norms and try our hardest to just fit in. Please don't. You were not sent here to be a clone or a copy and paste. Father loves you, your confidence, your sass, and your uniqueness. We all know how much we adore to see that little girl in the tutu and wellies who has obviously dressed herself, with the lipstick smudge across her face; it makes us smile. Our soul inside is screaming out, "You go, girl!" Be yourself and love it. We have stuffed down this same internal cheerleader when it comes to ourselves. Being different goes much deeper than what we wear, how we look, or how we dress; it goes to the very core of who we are.

Over the years I have had people say to me, "You are just different, not like other people," and as a younger person, I took that comment negatively. Now I have learned to grow into the compliment and embrace it. I like to think that the "different" in me is the light of Christ as I strive to be more like Him. He never fit in or conformed; He stood up and stood out from the very moment of His birth. He was Jesus Christ and not just any other little boy growing up in that time. He was unique, and He embraced it.

"As you dare to be different, your exemplary conduct will not go unnoticed. Although you will be tried and tested, your faithful adherence to the Lord's standards will be seen as a beacon in the night to those around you."[63]

How can we be different from others around us? How can we stand out as a beacon of light in our own homes and families as well as in the wider world we influence around us?

Speech is one thing that easily makes us stand out: the language you choose to avoid, the way you choose to speak about others. Taking time to notice people, smile, or just give a greeting can also make you stand out, along with the way you care for people, serve in the Church, asking for a blessing on your food, and so much more.

My dear mother-in-law (Jude) was an incredible example to me of being different and not being afraid of who she was. "You are incredible; everyone else can see it. Why can't you?" she once said to me, and it stuck. She was also an amazing example of a mother who loved and lived the gospel for her four sons. She would leave her scriptures out and open on the table after her morning study until the boys all got up, and they knew she was different from other Mums. She would also do her personal prayer with her bedroom door open, hoping that her children might happen upon her and see that she prayed personally to her Father in Heaven. Consider for a moment how you might show those in your home how you are different to the world.

What changes could you make?

---

63. Staheli, "Achieving Your Potential," 60.

> Let us dare to be different from the ways of the world when its ways are not the ways of God. In a world troubled with selfish greed, dishonesty, and dishonor, let us set ourselves on a higher path, striving to develop and strengthen the qualities of unselfish service with wholehearted effort, dependability, honesty, morality, and every other good attribute that would lead us to integrity of character.[64]

There have been several times when I might have been given the wrong change in a shop, charged the wrong price or my child has managed to leave the store still in the possession of a toy or a Cadbury Creme Egg that I was not aware of. I have taken it back and been honest, correcting the error, only to have the staff in the shop bemused that I have done it. "People just don't do that" and "Honesty is in short supply" are some of the things I have been told. What a sorry state of affairs. Being honest in our dealings is the most amazing way to stand out, and it restores others' hope in humankind.

We can choose not to be like Laman and Lemuel (the world) and to instead be more like Nephi as we choose not to murmur and to be of good cheer. It is easy to have a good moan and be fed up, but what an amazing way to be different as we stand up and find joy even in the darkest times, even when it rains. I love to see our ducks when it begins to rain; they find incredible joy in it. They run out of their house, not into it, and seemingly dance around. So look for your silver linings; don't murmur. Have a sunny disposition, and you will be different from the world, for sure.

The way we dress shows how we are different. This might mean that we let our creativity and quirkiness go crazy and wear things that are maybe not "fashionable" or "trendy" but are what makes us happy. Wellies and a tutu might not be the right outfit, but have fun! We can also be different as we dress with respect for our bodies and the covenants that we have made. When we wear our Sunday best on the Sabbath and don't rush to change, we are being different and showing that the Sabbath day is different and special to us.

When we serve, we show how different we are when we stop and help a neighbour, when we minister to those in our care, and when we

---

64. Delbert L. Stapley, "Good Habits Develop Good Character," *Ensign*, Nov. 1974, 21.

do random acts of kindness for our fellow man or woman. This is also a great way to show you are different in your community.

President David O. McKay quoted, "We sow our thoughts, and we reap our actions; we sow our actions, and we reap our habits; we sow our habits, and we reap our characters; we sow our characters, and we reap our destiny."[65] This is so true, as being different and being unique does start in the mind. Having a kind mind will lead to showing kindness and will lead us to become a kind person. How have your thoughts today been different? As a woman of great faith, realising your potential for good can help you choose to live and love your differences, help you showcase who you really are, and also helps others see the good in you that Father sees.

"Dare to be different. Be a pioneer. Be a leader. Be the kind of woman who in the face of adversity will continue to embrace life and walk fearlessly toward the challenge."[66]

Being different does require that you become a leader rather than a follower; it requires a moment's pause in a situation to work out how you should behave or what you should do in that very second and how that choice might change the course of your life. When people comment that you are different, thank them and tell them why. Tell them you are different because you KNOW you are a child of God, you know His plan, and that because you know that He loves you, you want to show Him just how much you love Him back.

You need to "dare to be more than ordinary. Dare to be extraordinary."[67] Do not be afraid to be the greatest you can be and an incredible, unique, and different woman of faith. No two of us are the same. This week really embrace, enjoy, and practice being different. Let out the inner voice shouting to you, "You go girl! You've got this!"

---

65. Stapley, "Good Habits," 20, quoting from C. A. Hall, *The Home Book of Quotations* [New York, NY: Dodd, Mead & Company,1935], 845.

66. Attributed to Oprah Winfrey in John Davis, Oprah Winfrey: 50 Best Quotes, Teachings and Secrets to Success by Oprah Winfrey (CreateSpace, 2016).

67. Attributed to Imania Margria.

9
Lose Yourself in Service

There is a phrase that I am not sure is one of my own making or something I have heard, but it says, "Give service at your earliest inconvenience." This has become a mantra for me. People's needs cannot be scheduled or planned. Some service is easier to factor into your week, and should be, but the most meaningful and wonderful service we will give is at our earliest inconvenience.

It will mean missing out on something else—it will make other plans tricky or even require them to be canceled—but this service will always stay with you. I have had many AMAZING opportunities to serve and to feel that I was able to share the love of our Father in Heaven. These experiences have been special and even sacred. They have helped me understand the concept of ministering and being His hands here on the earth as I have been able to drop everything and serve. I have also been blessed enough to be on the receiving end of this pure Christlike service, and I have seen how it has blessed my life and that of my family.

One occasion always stands out to me. When I was six months pregnant with my second child, my husband was working on his finals at university, and I was heading to pick up a young woman on my way to church for youth night. We were busy; we had a toddler, and life was pretty chaotic most days. When I arrived to collect her, there was an ambulance on the drive, and it was apparent that the dad was in a bad way. I was able to walk into the home, tell the mum to go with Dad, and then stand in for her and care for her six children, my toddler, and two HUGE dogs. My husband was able to go and support the mum at the hospital! It was what was needed at that moment, and within thirty-six hours, an army of sisters, family, and dinner and cleaning schedules were in place to support them over the next few weeks as the family needed. We were able to ensure that the family felt loved in the darkest of moments. Serve when you are needed, not when it suits you. Your service will make a difference and bless the lives of others; however, serving also means that your life is blessed—it's a win-win! I am not exceptional or special for serving in this way; it was a blessing to me, and I learned a lot.

Women of great faith serve each and every day in their homes, their families, their workplaces, their wards, their stakes, and the temples, to name but a few places. We have the incredible blessing of having a specific assignment for just a handful of sisters that we can minister to as Christ would. He loved, taught, prayed for, comforted, and blessed those around Him (see Acts 10:38). We are also blessed to know that other sisters in our ward have been specifically assigned through revelation to minister to our needs. His plan is for us to love others whilst we are loved too—what a perfect plan.

Service isn't always physical; it is often spiritual or emotional. It can be as simple as saying a prayer for someone, adding their name to the temple prayer roll, or sending a message. Great, big acts of service are incredible and so helpful, but the simple, quiet, and unconditional love of small acts mean the most, and their loving embrace can last the longest.

"The best way to find yourself is to lose yourself in the service of others."[68]

As we serve, we discover our true and happiest selves, we discover who we really are, and we find joy. If you are feeling low, depressed, or disillusioned, this is the very moment you NEED to serve, and you need to do it NOW! You will find great joy and happiness and will shine the light of Christ into the middle of your own personal storm.

How have you served today or this week? Create a list. It may be long, but try to focus on not just who you served or when you served

68. Attributed to Mahatma Gandhi.

but on what attitude with which you serve. The attitude that we have as we serve makes an incredible difference. Service with a bad attitude will not bring love to the recipient or joy into your own life. Service and the willingness to serve our brothers and sisters is an important part of our eternal progression. We grow by serving others and by allowing others to serve us.

The lyrics to this beautiful hymn should be our mantra and the song by which we live and assess our daily service. I like to try to use it as a metaphorical checklist and tick as many as I can each day; it is not easy, and life often gets in the way of serving or even seeing the need to serve. Pray for opportunities to serve and the ability to identify those in need and those the Lord would have you share His love with today.

> Have I done any good in the world today?
> Have I helped anyone in need?
> Have I cheered up the sad and made someone feel glad?
> If not, I have failed indeed.
> Has anyone's burden been lighter today
> Because I was willing to share?
> Have the sick and the weary been helped on their way?
> When they needed my help was I there?[69]

The hymn then suggests that if you haven't achieved at least one of those in your day, you need to get up, back out of bed, and "do something more"! It says that doing good (service) is a pleasure and that our joy will be beyond measure. What a wonderful promise. Keep this song in mind each day this week as you seek out chances to have more joy and pleasure.

Have you ever noticed that some people just love to serve? They are first to offer help in the ward, in the family, and in the wider community. They don't feel like any task is too small or too big, and they love to roll up their sleeves and go to work! These people have found the treasure of service; they know that by living and loving and serving as the Saviour would, their own life is filled with incredible joy. This doesn't mean that their problems have disappeared or that they

---

69. "Have I Done Any Good?," *Hymns*, 223.

have no hardship. It enables them to put challenges and hardship into perspective; there is always someone worse off than you are.

Maybe these joyous servers have this primary song ringing in their ears and it helps them.

"When we're helping, we're happy, And we sing as we go; And we like to help mother [or insert someone's name], For we all love her so. Tra la la la la la la."[70]

When you go to serve next, maybe you can sing along as a reminder that service is love, it is charity, and it is the pure love of Christ. Through service we can learn more about this most incredible gift to be like Him and to become more as we strive to serve everyone we meet. We can do small acts of service or even service at home, such as indexing, a phone call, a WhatsApp message, or a letter. Your act of kindness may be delivering cakes via knock-door run or the simple kindness and service of speaking to someone and actually listening. When President Gordon B. Hinckley was on his mission, he felt despondent and wondered why he even was bothering; his father wrote this note in his letter: "Forget yourself and go to work."[71] That is what our Father in Heaven would say to us when we feel uninspired or lethargic about serving. He would say, "Forget your hard things for now, and get busy and go to work!"

As a women of great faith, you serve diligently within the walls of your own homes, wards, and community. You will seek out, pray for, and find joy in serving your fellow man and woman. You seek the happiness that you know can be yours as you serve. You want to be more like Father and your elder brother Jesus Christ as you learn to minister as They do. Women of great faith know that ministering is an essential part of Father's plan to care for, love, and support the sisters and families in your ward; therefore, YOU can choose to be His minister.

---

70. "When We're Helping," *Children's Songbook*, 198b.

71. Bryant S. Hinckley, quoted in Gordon B. Hinckley, "Taking the Gospel to Britain: A Declaration of Vision, Faith, Courage, and Truth," *Ensign*, Jul. 1987.

10
Keep Your Testimony Burning Brightly

Your testimony is one of the most precious but potentially fragile things that you have. The adversary would love to destroy it, chip away at it, and damage it. Your testimony is the fuel that drives your ability to be a woman of great faith, as your knowing that He is your Saviour, that your Father in Heaven loves you, and that this is His gospel restored to the earth helps you make decisions for good each and every day. Your testimony helps you make the right choices even in the hardest days because you KNOW that He will make everything right.

Your testimony is never complete or finished. To enable it to be strong, you need to keep building it and fortifying it. "Gaining a testimony is like building a fire. Just as we need to add wood to keep a fire burning, we must pray, repent, serve others, study the scriptures, and keep the commandments to help our testimonies grow."[72] When we do these precious things, we fuel our fires and we create a brighter and more beautiful testimony.

The analogy of fire is perfect for testimonies, as fire can easily be spread but can also be hard to start, even when you have all the right fuel. It can also go out without warning. On the other hand, even the smallest embers can create a spark that can cause a forest fire. When we have a testimony of the gospel of Jesus Christ, when we have this

---

72. "Let Your Testimony Burn Bright," *Ensign* or *Liahona*, Feb. 2015, 6.

beautiful fire in our souls, our testimony can give us comfort and warmth just as a fire burning in the hearth can; that fire will also attract others who want to feel its warmth and comfort. Your testimony, when shared, will do that; it may just provide comfort and warmth, or the embers may ignite a small glow in others, the potential for a fire in their souls, and a great testimony. Fire is amazing. We can enjoy the warmth of others' fires and allow the glow and light of Christ to touch our souls, but as anyone who has ever stood next to a fire knows, without turning around, only one side of you is warmed; you need to be forever moving and repositioning to endure so that you are warmed all over. This is the same with our testimonies. We cannot just stand still and stay where we are; we need to move, progress, and reposition all the time. When you take this fabulous fire of testimony into your soul, you can begin to fully appreciate its beauty and greatness.

Some of you may be familiar with a song, often sung in primary school[73], called "Magic Penny," or, "Love Is Something If You Give It Away" (Malvina Reynolds). This was one of my favourites, but I want to switch the word "Love" with "Your Testimony." "[Your Testimony] Is something If You Give It Away." We do not actually give our testimony away, but we do gift it to those that we share it with. Yes, it is a gift—a gift we give and share and others receive. As we gift it to others and share it around just as the song says, we end up receiving more, it grows, it strengthens, and most of all, it blesses others.

In a regional conference in the UK, Elder M. Russell Ballard taught us that our testimonies are our most precious gift:

> Let your prayers to your Father in Heaven include a desire that He place one of His children in your pathway, so you can share what you now know is true . . . . There can be no greater gift that any one of us can give.[74]

Do you seek to fuel your fire of testimony by finding people to share it with?

Have you prayed for someone to be placed in your path?

---

73. Elementary School.

74. Rachel Sterzer Gibson, "Today is President Ballard's 94th birthday. Here are 12 of his quotes from the past year," *Church News*, Oct. 8. 2022, from Message to Latter-day Saints in England, Ireland, Scotland, and Wales, Oct. 31, 2021.

When we are asked to share our testimony with people outside of a testimony meeting, many of us shudder and worry that it will just be too hard; we decide for others that they won't want to hear what we have to say, but in doing so, we actually remove their agency! When you share your testimony, it doesn't require standing and sharing the entirety of your testimony, and it doesn't have to start with "Dear Brothers and Sisters" and end in an Amen. It is snippets that we share, stories and experiences that we can testify about things that we know and that are appropriate to share. It might involve talking with a friend who is sick and saying you will pray for them. Fairly easy, right? But to testify, we need to take it a little further. You can tell them that you know that people can be healed and comforted through the power of prayer—again, not too hard, but in that additional sentence, you have testified, you have triggered a spark, you have told them that you have faith, that you are a woman of great faith, and that you believe this will help them. You can even take it one step further by inviting them to pray with you or by offering to arrange for a priesthood blessing for them. This is a simplified explanation, but when you talk about the gospel with a friend, colleague, or anyone who is listening, try to think, *I said it. Now I need to testify of it!* The hardest bit is the first bit—saying it—so don't ever miss out on the chance to testify of it.

People love to hear stories, and that is what our testimony is—a series of stories and experiences that we have collected that have taught us that God is there, that He answers our prayers, and that this is His gospel restored to the earth for the latter days. When you seek to share your testimony, you will find it incredible just how easy it is. Set yourself a goal to be a testifier and to be able to seek out those with whom you can share your fire. That said, don't forget to look within the walls of your own home first. If you have a testimony-building experience, make sure you tell your children/family; if you pray and a prayer is answered, testify. Tell them that you prayed and that He answered your prayers and you know He is waiting to answer theirs. If you are healed because of a blessing, tell them, and let them know that they too can be healed when they are sick if they are faithful. If you pay tithing and you see the blessings as you make ends meet, tell them, and let them know the blessings you have received, and let them know that they too can receive great blessings from paying tithes and offerings, and finally, when you are in the temple serving the Lord, come home and tell them about it; testify of the feelings you have felt and of the service that you have done, and let them know that they too can enjoy these blessings when they are eleven and onwards as they serve in the temple. This list could really go on and on, but we need to make sure that to have the fires of testimony burning brightly in our home, we testify daily to our children/families about little things, and often, bearing our testimony every single day, which in turn strengthens our own testimonies. Women of great faith testify at every opportunity; they never take the credit but openly see the Lord in their lives and His influence in their day. They openly celebrate His part in their lives by testifying of it to those they love and those within their sphere of influence.

"Testimony—real testimony, born of the Spirit and confirmed by the Holy Ghost—changes lives."[75]

One way we can really stoke up the fires of our testimony is to testify to ourselves! That might seem like a strange idea, but we can keep a journal, either in a book or maybe in the notes on our phone, of every time we testify or want to and chickened out—it happens! Make a note of it. What did you feel? What did you say or want to say? How do you know it? Doing this, we are recording important things, things that are almost our own personal scripture, and we can refer to it often to lift ourselves.

Take the time on fasting testimony Sunday to get up and testify; set an example for your family as a woman of great faith. Don't find an excuse not to; just decide that is what you will do each month, and do it! You don't need to have some clever story or witty anecdote; share one thing you know, and testify of it, and then invite others to receive the same knowledge, blessing, or experience. Short, sweet, and powerful make the most effective testimonies. Last month I was inspired to get up and share my testimony, but I didn't manage to, and the meeting came to a close. I was unsure what to do with the prompting, so I wrote down what I wanted to say and messaged it to the sisters I

75. M. Russell Ballard, "Pure Testimony," *Ensign* or *Liahona*, Nov. 2004, 40.

ministered to (who were all missing from that meeting), and they each replied letting me know that was just what they needed to hear that day. Testify; it has incredible power.

We are taught to "stand as witnesses of God at all times and in all things, and in all places" (Mosiah 18:9). This means every day, everywhere, and every way. Testifying and sharing our testimony will become the most natural part of our conversations; as we do it more, we lose the fear that we might offend or upset someone as we share who we really are. Women of great faith choose to stand, speak, and testify of Christ, and we choose to burn bright, not hiding our light under bushels. We set them alight with our flames!

11
Great Latter-day Work

President Wilford Woodruff observed that those women "who are called to take part in the great latter-day work . . . should be . . . women of faith, valiant for the truth, . . . women of integrity to God" who do "not permit houses and land, gold and silver, nor any of this world's goods to draw [them] aside from pursuing the great object which God has sent [them] to perform."[76]

So what is that "great latter-day work"? If we are to achieve this, we need to know what is expected of us. Is there a checklist?

We read in the quote above that we should be women of faith; let's be women of great faith. We should be valiant for truth, be always true and courageous as we stand for that truth, and we should be women of integrity, and not just integrity but integrity to God. What does that mean? We need to be truthful and honourable, upright before our God, our fellow men and women, and ourselves. Evaluating the way we treat ourselves is essential as we choose to grow.

We were saved for this time; we were saved for the latter days. What we were needed for was now. When I think about the fact that this is MY time and the time that I was designed to be here for, I then reflect on other points and eras in time (I love history), and then I very quickly conclude that I would have really struggled to live at a different time! Your life here and now isn't an accident of birth but rather part of Father's beautiful design, just like Esther's having "come to the kingdom for such a time as this" (Esther 4:14). This is the exact

76. Wilford Woodruff, *Deseret News: Semi-Weekly*, Oct. 18, 1881, 1.

time. You are made for now; you have the strength and ability to live in these latter days and to love, guide, and support the youth that you influence as they embrace their missions in the latter days too.

Our beloved Prophet Russell M. Nelson teaches us, "My dear sisters, we need *you*!" Is it only me here that visualises a World War I recruitment poster? The battle may be different, but this was what President Nelson was doing—recruiting us sisters, women of great faith, to be a part of the Lord's battalion in the latter days. He goes on to say, "We 'need *your* strength, *your* conversion, *your* conviction, *your* ability to lead, *your* wisdom, and *your* voices.' We simply cannot gather Israel without you."[77]

Amazing, and mind-blowing all in one sentence, we are needed, and without us (that's you and me), the gathering of Israel, part of the Father's plan and a step in the Second Coming of our elder brother Jesus Christ, will be hampered; it will be made harder if YOU don't play your part! President Nelson said in that same address, "I'm extending a prophetic plea to you, the women of the Church, to shape the future by helping to gather scattered Israel."[78] So here it is; this is one of the things that you need to do for your great latter-day work.

What does it mean to gather Israel? What does that look like to you today? In the same conference talk, President Nelson invited us to enlist and take our place in the Lord's battalion; he initially extended the invitation to the youth of the Church, but his invitation is just as relevant to you and me. He taught that the gathering was taking place here on Earth and through the veil in the spirit world and that gathering Israel is "*the greatest* challenge, *the greatest* cause, and *the greatest* work on earth today" (Russell M. Nelson, "Sisters' Participation in the Gathering of Israel," 69)!

He gave us four steps to help in our task within this battalion to help gather Israel:

- Take a social media fast or break for ten days. We may have all taken part in this at the time; however, he didn't say that it was a one-off! Fasting is a part of our regular worship, so

77. Russell M. Nelson, "Sisters' Participation in the Gathering of Israel," *Ensign* or *Liahona*, Nov. 2018, 70.

78. Russell M. Nelson, "Sisters' Participation in the Gathering of Israel," 69.

maybe we could choose to take a regular break from social media, say once a year. What about doing it this week?

- Read the Book of Mormon every day. He didn't say how much or when and where; reading from it was his guidance, and you and I know that each person's schedule varies so much. Some of us may have thirty minutes a day to sit back and enjoy our study; for others, it might be just two minutes in the car at the school pickup. This week find out when you have time to fit in this wonderful study, and remember that the Book of Mormon was preserved for you and for now, so it's probably exactly what you need to know!
- Attend the temple regularly. What your life looks like right now and your proximity to the nearest temple will have an impact; a regular pattern could be once a week, once a month, or once a year. Just establish a plan and prepare and plan to go. When temple attendance is hard or if you don't have a current recommend, you can work towards being able to attend and in the meantime establish a pattern of temple work through family history and genealogy, ensuring that you submit the work to be done in the temple.
- "Participate fully in Relief Society."[79] What does it mean to fully participate? Do you attend your Sunday Relief Society meetings? Some people are currently not in a position to attend, as they have callings in Primary or with the youth, but the rest of us should be there, and not just attend but, as the directive says, we should participate fully. Study and prepare for the class, take part, and choose to find upliftment in the words said by the teacher. Do you attend the weekday activities? Busy lives can make this hard, but we should be there building relationships with our fellow sisters and fellowshipping one another. Do you minister as the Saviour would? We should all have a ministering assignment, and we need to evaluate how well we minister. How could we be a better minister? Do our sisters know of the Saviour's love because

79. Russell M. Nelson, "Sisters' Participation in the Gathering of Israel," 69–70.

of us? Making Relief Society a joy and a pleasure will help us participate fully in the program and its associated blessings.

"Are we giving our all to the Lord without reservation? Are we sacrificing of our time and talents so the rising generation can learn to love the Lord and keep His commandments? Are we ministering both to those around us and to those we are assigned with care and with diligence— sacrificing time and energy that could be used in other ways? Are we living the two great commandments—to love God and to love His children?"[80]

To be prepared for the service required for the latter days, we need to follow the four steps from President Nelson and readjust our focus; everyone has times when things become fuzzy or lost in the blur of the day, but as we consciously choose to follow these steps, we will be blessed, and we will be able to become the women of great faith that Heavenly Father knows we are.

"Women of God can never be like women of the world. The world has enough women who are tough; we need women who are tender. There are enough women who are coarse; we need women who are kind. There are enough women who are rude; we need women who are refined. We have enough women of fame and fortune; we need more women of faith. We have enough greed; we need more goodness. We have enough vanity; we need more virtue. We have enough popularity; we need more purity."[81]

You are needed, you are wanted, you are an essential part, and Father knows that you will do great things. Maybe this week you could study about the gathering of Israel in greater depth and determine what you are doing well and what you need to do. You can try to include the things you need to do in short- and long-term goals and plans.

80. Cristina B. Franco, "The Joy of Unselfish Service," *Ensign* or *Liahona*, Nov. 2018, 56.

81. Margaret D. Nadauld, "The Joy of Womanhood," Nov. 2000, 15.

As a woman of great faith, you embrace the teachings of the prophet about the latter days and strive to play your part in the gathering of Israel. You share your light and set an example in your homes and families and strive to do the things He needs you to do.

12
Endure and Have Faith

"Be strong, be brave, be true, endure."[82]

When I think of endurance, I think of things that last a long time, that don't wear out or wear down easily; I also think of hard things and challenges. This is very much the case for each and every one of us, as we are told,

"Look unto me, and endure to the end, and ye shall live; for unto him that endureth to the end will I give eternal life." (3 Nephi 15:9)

We must endure through this mortal experience. It is but a glimpse into our eternal existence; however, in the hard and challenging times, it can feel endless and beyond our abilities and our capacity to see it through. This is why we need to not just endure but to have faith whilst we do so; we need to always have our celestial radar on as we remind ourselves of where we are heading, that this is but a short time, and we can endure it.

It seems quite simple and clear as we study the gospel and especially the plan of salvation and the Restoration that those who endure, and stay loyal to their covenants, will receive eternal life. It's a solid promise and one that has clear guidance and boundaries.

So what does enduring look like? One latter-day prophet taught us:

82. Attributed to Dave Eggers.

> I say to the Latter-day Saints, no amount of knowledge, no amount of testimony, no amount of sealing in the temples of God to our wives and children will save us; but the keeping of the commandments of God, being honest in our dealings with God and with our fellow men, paying our tithing, obeying the Word of Wisdom and doing our duty as Latter-day Saints— these are the things, and the only things that will save us.[83]

Just as the pioneers on the plains kept going and placed one foot in front of the other, day after day, in the worst of circumstances and exhausted from all the pressures they faced, this is how we as modern-day pioneers need to proceed. Day in and day out, we need to start over and keep trying to do what we know we should do, resetting and starting again on the things that may have been dropped along the way or just put down as we were at capacity for a while. We need to lift ourselves and those around us even on the hardest days and just keep going, keep trying, and gradually edging closer to our promised land, the land of eternal life and paradisiacal glory. There is a Disney character called Dory, whom some of you may be familiar with. Her mantra has become mine to "Just keep swimming," although she cannot remember why or to what end; her resolve to just keep going can be a reminder to us that should be our mantra, but we know the end. We know our destination. We know why we want to get there and whom we want to take with us! This is because we have faith, understanding, and knowledge that we can lean on and depend upon. This concept to just keep swimming can give us great resolve and the ability to reach our goals, even if we have to tread water sometimes to help us through the hard times. I am often heard saying when people might ask how I am "Upright and staggering forward" is my response, as there are many days when jumping from bed with a spring in our step isn't possible and just placing that one step in front of the other is all we can do—but you did it!

"Blessed are they who are faithful and endure, . . . for they shall inherit eternal life." (Doctrine and Covenants 50:5)

---

83. Heber J. Grant, general conference address, Oct. 7, 1900, Historical General Conferences, https://historicalgeneralconferences.weebly.com/1900-october.html

We are taught that we will be blessed; I believe that this is a mortal and an eternal blessing. As we live the gospel of Jesus Christ and exercise faith, even great faith, in His plan, we will receive blessings. Count them and cherish them.

Brigham young shared the commandment given by our Saviour Jesus Christ:

> "If ye love me, keep my commandments."
>
> How long? For a day? Keep the commandments of the Lord for a week? Observe and do his will for a month or a year? There is no promise to any individual, that I have any knowledge of, that he shall receive the reward of the just, unless he is faithful to the end.[84]

This is endurance; it is our resolve and our commitment to do His will and His work until our very final moments of mortality.

We have, however, been given a great and incredible support as we trudge through mortality and as we strive to endure and have faith—that is the guiding hand and supportive arms of our dearest comforter and friend, the Holy Ghost.

"One of the great privileges of the gift of the Holy Ghost is a magnifying power, strength, or ability beyond what we are normally capable of doing."[85]

I love this quote and also this incredible book by David Butler; it taught me so much about the wonderful gift my older brother gave to me in the Holy Ghost. He really meant what he said to the Apostles: "And I will pray the Father, and he shall give you another Comforter, that he may abide with you for ever; Even the Spirit of truth; whom the world cannot receive, because it seeth him not, neither knoweth him: but ye know him; for he dwelleth with you, and shall be in you" (John 14:16, 17).

A comforter that we will have always and forever, that will dwell with us, but we need to know Him. This means being in tune with

84. Brigham Young, in *Journal of Discourses*, 13:36.

85. David Butler, *Spirit: The Gift That Connects You to Heaven* (Salt Lake City, UT: Deseret Book, 2020).

Him, and we achieve that as we tune out the interference of the world and worldly things, control the natural man, and focus on listening to His promptings.

President James E. Faust taught, "The adversary tries to smother [us] with a multitude of loud, persistent, persuasive, and appealing voices." These voices will lead us away from the joy of the gospel. President Faust added that we must "filter out the static generated by Satan."[86]

If we're to listen to the voice of the Spirit, how do we know that we're tuning in to His guidance? "President Gordon B. Hinckley (1910–2008) said that we can know by asking ourselves, 'Does it persuade one to do good, to rise, to stand tall, to do the right thing, to be kind, to be generous? Then it is of the Spirit of God.'"[87]

So we need to endure, we need to be faithful to the very end, but we need to do it hand in hand with the Holy Ghost with an eternal perspective and make sure we tune out the interference that can cloud our judgments and make it hard to progress the right way. I love the following quote; it helps me to endure, not just with faith but also a sense of humour (which I think is essential):

"Everything will be all right in the end. If it's not all right, it is not yet the end." (Original quote attributed to Fernando Sabino)

Everything really will be all right in the end. The end is eternal life with those we love, in paradisiacal glory, so since we are not there yet, let's just know that as long as we keep trying, we will get there.

As a woman of great faith, you can achieve all that Father has planned for you. You can rely on the Comforter to get you through this life and lean on your cheerleaders. Women of faith not only endure for themselves; they bring along those they love, edging them closer and closer to their own gift of eternal life. Women of great faith also offer comfort, love, and support to others on their own journey

86. James E. Faust, "Voice of the Spirit," First Presidency Message, *Ensign* or *Liahona*, Jun. 2006.

87. Eric B. Murdock, "Tune In to the Spirit," *New Era*, Jun. 2014, 11.

of endurance, and they do so with a smile on their face and a skip in their step. We know it's hard, and we know we have to endure, but we will only have this mortal experience once, so let's try to enjoy it! "In all of living have much fun and laughter. Life is to be enjoyed, not just endured."[88]

---

88. Gordon B. Hinckley, "Stand True and Faithful," *Ensign*, May 1996, 94.

13
Your Noble Birthright

Women of great faith have many facets shining like the beautiful diamonds that they are and embrace womanhood. When you know who you are as well as whose you are, you can stand tall, with confidence, and shine. You need not say anything or explain yourself, as the nobility of your divine birthright can be seen in your composure full of reverence, peace, and faith.

> You are literally spirit daughters of Deity, "offspring of exalted parents" with a divine nature and an eternal destiny. You received your first lessons in the world of spirits from your heavenly parents.
>
> You have been sent to earth to "prove" yourselves. . . . You are treasured children of the promise. If you will keep the Lord's statutes and commandments and hearken to His voice, He has promised that He will make you high above the nations in name and honour and praise.[89]

"Daughter of a King" by Jenny Phillips is one of my favourite songs. I would love for you all to listen to it now, as it talks beautifully about our noble birthright.

In the song Jenny poses a series of questions and gives us many things to think about. She asks if we know who we are and whether He knows who we are, whether we realise that He hears the very pleadings of our heart. She goes on to remind us that He knows about every piece of sand on the shore reminding us how significant we are

89. Julie B. Beck, "You Have a Noble Birthright," *Ensign* or *Liahona*, May 2006, 106–7.

and also the HUGE reminder, which is that He believes in me and you.

Just last night I had the privilege to be with my daughter and son-in-law as they welcomed their first child into the world. It was a little crazy, and there were some complications. I was humbled to see my son-in-law turn to the Lord in prayer every time there was a worry and plead with all his heart. I saw miracles shower down on that hospital room in answer to the pleadings of his heart and mine.

You don't need to wonder; you don't need to question—you know. Father is there, and He knows you, the young and gentle spirit that dwelt with Him before, the mortal you, the fighter, the finisher, the one that is striving, and the one that is resetting every day a course back home to Him. He also knows your eternal you, your capacity and potential, how great you already are, and how marvelous you will become. You also need to remember that just as we believe in Him and in the mission and ministry of His Son Jesus Christ, He believes in you too, in your mission and ministry.

Reading the words *noble birthright* conjures up a number of thoughts in my mind. I love history (as I may have mentioned), and in British history, we have the nobles. They are the elite, the ones who have everything and whose connection to their father gives them the ability to thrive, own lands, rule, and reign. However, the term *noble* can also mean having, showing, or coming from personal qualities that people admire (such as honesty, generosity, courage, etc.). I believe that we, as women of great faith, are both of these descriptions of the noble: we are elite as daughters of a King, a child of God, and we have the capacity to have EVERYTHING in the eternities when we come of age and have moved on from this mortal realm. We will have the capacity one day to become heirs and become just like the Father. We spend this life perfecting the noble attributes that help us embrace our birthright.

Once, when asked if I had one wish, what would it be, my answer startled. "I wish that everyone knew and understood that they are a child of God!" Can you imagine just how incredible the world would then be, if everyone we met really knew it and believed it? I guess that is probably what heaven looks like. If everyone believed and knew this truth, it would change everything. I then reflected and realised that I know it and believe it, so it really should change me fundamentally. If I know it's true for me, then I know that everyone I meet is also a precious child of God with a noble birthright, so I realised that I needed to work on myself so that I could treat everyone how they deserve to be treated. I know that they are special even if they don't. If, as women of great faith, we make this change in our thoughts, it really can change our lives and elevate our relationship with others and our Father in Heaven. We will learn to love deeper and with an unconditional love for our fellow man. It will help us love those we have custodianship over, with a new and exciting passion, as we hope they come to realise their worth.

We talked earlier in the book about how precious we are to Father and just how much He loves us. As we reflect upon our noble status this week, I want us to really digest and consider what this knowledge means to us; maybe journal your thoughts. I would also like to challenge you to teach and talk about this incredible truth with your families and prayerfully consider who else in your sphere of influence would benefit to know that you believe that all of us are precious to our Father in Heaven and are literally His children. We teach this principle from the very moment our children begin primary, but do we properly understand what it means and just how incredible that knowledge is?

God, the architect of this earth, the Almighty, is your Father.

> You youth of the noble birthright are not perfect yet. None of us are. So you, along with the rest of us, are very grateful for the Atonement of the Savior, which provides full forgiveness as you truly repent. You also know that your stay here in mortality is relatively brief. In time, each of you will graduate from this frail existence and move on to the next world.
>
> Judgment Day awaits each of us. I know that "the keeper of the gate is the Holy One of Israel; and he employeth no servant there" (2 Nephi 9:41). Yes, each of us will have a personal interview with Jesus Christ. Each day on earth gives you time and opportunity to prepare for that interview.[90]

Sister Ardeth G. Kapp teaches us

90. Russell M. Nelson, "What Will You Choose?" *Ensign* or *Liahona*, Jan. 2015.

> I wish I could sit with each one of you in the swing on my back porch this time of year, just as the sun is going down.
>
> It is so much fun to listen to the crickets. Those who have trained themselves to listen well can distinguish between a cricket's love call, a danger signal, and other messages that simply say, "I'm here."
>
> Did you know that crickets actually listen with ears they have located on their knees? When I'm on my knees, I try to listen. . . .
>
> Do you know you are literally youth of the noble birthright? Young women, I plead with you, find your own back porch, away from the demanding, loud voices of the world. Learn to really listen—not to the crickets, but to the constant whisperings of the Spirit with its messages of hope prompting you each step of the way on your road to the celestial kingdom.[91]

As women of great faith, let us embrace the noble, be loyal to the royal, and look forward to the glorious day when we can receive our birthright. Let us be women who know, who testify, and who teach that we are all beautiful, precious, equal, and important children of a loving Father in Heaven. Let us have faith and direction in our lives as we strive to be noble in our actions and attributes. Let us always remember that He knows and understands us, and as women of great faith, let us strive every day to strengthen that bond with our Father in Heaven.

"We need women who have a bedrock understanding of the doctrine of Christ and who will use that understanding to teach and help raise a sin-resistant generation. We need women who can detect deception in all of its forms. We need women who know how to access the power that God makes available to covenant keepers and who express their beliefs with confidence and charity. We need women who have the courage and vision of our Mother Eve. . . . step forward! Take your rightful and needful place in your home, in your community, and in the kingdom of God."[92]

---

91. Ardeth G. Kapp, "A Time for Hope," *Ensign*, Nov. 1986, 87, 89.

92. Russell M. Nelson, "A Plea to My Sisters," 97.

14
Go Forward with Conviction

"A conviction that you are a daughter of God gives you a feeling of comfort in your self-worth. It means that you can find strength in the balm of Christ. It will help you meet the heartaches and challenges with faith and serenity."[93]

We are strong women on a journey. We are women who are daily standing for what we know to be true and moving forward with great faith towards our destiny. We are striving and trying and picking ourselves up, shaking off the dust, and trying again. So we are going forward, but do we do it with conviction?

When my son reported for his mission to the Provo Missionary Training Center, he was excited and embraced it with vigour. After six weeks he travelled to the France Lyon Mission, ready to serve. Within a few days we spoke, and it was apparent that he had realised he had a long way to go with his language skills; people would speak, and it bore almost no resemblance to the French he had learned in the MTC. I asked him to bear me his testimony in French, which he did, and I then explained about how far he had come in the last seven weeks. He could only see how far he had to go, and his confidence wobbled, but he needed to remind himself just how well he was doing. I sent him a picture of a tortoise, and it said, *Your speed doesn't matter.*

93. James E. Faust, "What It Means to Be a Daughter of God," *Ensign*, Nov. 1999, 102.

Forward is still forward. This is relevant to each of us. Where were you a week ago, a month ago, a year ago? How far have you come? The distance is almost irrelevant as long as it is forward. In fact, even if we stood still for a moment, that was still forward. Once my missionary recommitted to showing faith and having confidence in his abilities with the Lord by his side, he flourished and learned to love, even adore, the French language. It is actually more like his first language now, as even after returning home, he chooses to pray in French, and his inner voice is now French.

> Let us rejoice in the knowledge that although we are to stand with courage as we travel through mortality and even through our trials, God will not leave us without His guidance and sustaining power.
>
> May we go forward with our righteous convictions. May we walk in truth and in faith and in love. For if we will do so, we will be upheld and strengthened by the Lord: "Peace I leave with you, my peace I give unto you: not as the world giveth, give I unto you. Let not your heart be troubled, neither let it be afraid" (John 14:27).[94]

This is what it is to move forward with conviction, not just staggering forward by chance but by choice. Although, there are days when if I am upright and staggering forward, I will take that as a win!

What are our convictions? What even are convictions? I am reminded to consider the term *conviction* in a court of law; there is an accusation, and we are either convicted as guilty or not. If we had to stand accused of being a daughter of God, a faithful servant of His, a minister, and a mother in Zion, if we were accused of being a woman of great faith, would the evidence stack up to prove us guilty? I would hope so. I would hope that everything I do is evidence that I am striving to be all of those things and more. I would want to be able to say when accused of these things, "I am. I am guilty as charged."

However, I am not sure that when we are encouraged to move forward in our convictions, the law and the judicial systems are what are being talked about. Unless we consider the most important time of judgment, when we will be required to stand before our Saviour Jesus

---

94. Gordon B. Hinckley, "Living with Our Convictions," First Presidency Message, *Ensign*, Sept. 2001.

Christ. Will the evidence of our life, thoughts, and actions be enough for Him to see, will He know, that I am His? As the scripture says, will I have "received His image in [my countenance]?" (Alma 5:14).

The convictions that I think we need to have and develop are ones that will prove us, when needed, to our Father in Heaven and Jesus Christ as we acquire a state of mind in which we are free from doubt, in which we know who we are, where we are going, and why we want to be there. A mind that is great and full of knowledge and understanding that longs to dive into the scriptures and hear the prophet speak. Woman of great faith, that is you, and I have confidence in your testimony and certainty in the plan of salvation and our beloved Saviour. We choose to be as positive as possible in our daily lives as we try to steer ourselves away from doubt. We gain great satisfaction as we serve and love our fellow men and women as He would and serve in our homes and families with decisiveness and determination to help them have this same conviction and to travel forward with us to greatness.

When we choose to have true conviction in ourselves and His plan, we live a life full of purpose and choices with a resolve to always be better, stronger, and more. We are already great, and we need to remind ourselves that we are enough; however, we can always grow to be more like the Saviour and our Heavenly Parents. Moving forward with conviction is embracing the covenants we have made and rejoicing in them. Don't see them as a burden or a constant list of things we want to achieve. We need to know that each of these covenants is something that protects us and helps us stay safe; it is a piece of heaven in our daily lives. We need to live up to our covenants and achieve the greatness the Saviour has promised, each day resetting and refocusing as we try to keep moving forward, regardless of our speed. The speed at which we travel will also be greatly affected by our season in life. Look at your season and your moment, and make the very most of what you can whilst being realistic and allowing yourself to excel and see your forward progress.

> President Spencer W. Kimball made a profound prophecy about the impact that covenant-keeping women would have on the future of the Lord's Church. He prophesied: 'Much of the major growth

> that is coming to the Church in the last days will come because many of the good women of the world … will be drawn to the Church in large numbers. This will happen to the degree that the women of the Church reflect righteousness and articulateness in their lives and to the degree that the women of the Church are seen as distinct and different—in happy ways—from the women of the world.'
>
> My dear sisters, you who are our vital associates during this winding-up scene, the day that President Kimball foresaw is today. You are the women he foresaw! Your virtue, light, love, knowledge, courage, character, faith, and righteous lives will draw good women of the world, along with their families, to the Church in unprecedented numbers!
>
> We, your brethren, need your strength, your conversion, your conviction, your ability to lead, your wisdom, and your voices. The kingdom of God is not and cannot be complete without women who make sacred covenants and then keep them, women who can speak with the power and authority of God![95]

Without you, this work will struggle; it was designed with you in mind. He knew your special skills and attributes, and He planned with you that this was the time you would come and serve. He also knows that because of you, His gospel will move forward and that your righteous life as a woman of great faith will influence the world around you. Your convictions and passion will be what people see and want to follow. You were who President Kimball saw in that prophecy. Beautiful, powerful, incredible women of great faith, moving forward and doing it with great joy and happiness.

---

95. Russell M. Nelson, "A Plea to My Sisters," 96.

15
Becoming Creators and Builders

Women of great faith are creators; we create homes where the Spirit can dwell, and we create relationships and build those around us. Creativity comes naturally to many of us but in different forms and ways.

> We are to be creators in our own right—builders of an individual faith in God, faith in the Lord Jesus Christ, and faith in His Church.
>
> We are to build families and be sealed in holy temples. We are to build the Church and kingdom of God upon the earth. We are to prepare for our own divine destiny—glory, immortality, and eternal lives. These supernal blessings can all be ours, through our faithfulness.[96]

We, like Father and our elder brother Jesus Christ, are predisposed to create; we may not be creating whole worlds, but for those in our influence and families, it may well be the whole word to them! We can build homes that are secure and nurturing, places of safety and security, homes where the Spirit can dwell and we can all thrive. Being a builder and creator is an attribute of Christ, as He builds things and people up, whereas the adversary destroys and breaks things down. Women of great faith build and create as we look to the future mortally and eternally and look to our mansions in Heaven.

---

96. Russell M. Nelson, "The Creation," *Ensign*, May 2000, 86.

"There is strength and great capacity in the women of this Church. There is leadership and direction, a certain spirit of independence, and yet great satisfaction in being a part of this, the Lord's kingdom, and of working hand in hand with [holders of] the priesthood to move it forward."[97]

"God has given the women of this church a work to do in building his kingdom. That concerns all aspects of our great triad of responsibility—which is, first, to teach the gospel to the world; second, to strengthen the faith and build the happiness of the membership of the Church; and, third, to carry forward the great work of salvation for the dead."[98]

We will be able to not just build our individual homes but also the wards and stakes in which we live, building His kingdom right here in our own corner of the vineyard. We will also build His kingdom as we stand as witnesses and be missionaries and ministers, building the membership of the Church and participating in the gathering of Israel.

Women of great faith also create and build families, eternal families. We seek and support our posterity and lineage through family history and temple work, each person and name another link of strength in the wonderful eternal family we are building. Each block brings us closer to the celestial kingdom and all its wonders.

We can embrace the incredible gifts of creativity as we build gardens and nurture plants, growing flowers, vegetables, and fruits. We create homes and learn crafts and skills that beautify the places where we live. We create friendships and relationships that will support us, develop us, and build us to become better people; these friendships create support groups and alliances that we can depend on as we travel through this mortality. We can build and develop our minds, filling them with knowledge, which can in turn be the catalysts for many amazing creations.

97. Gordon B. Hinckley, "Women of the Church," *Ensign*, Nov. 1996, 67–8.

98. Gordon B. Hinckley, "Live Up to Your Inheritance," *Ensign*, Nov. 1983, 84.

In Primary we learn the song "The Wise Man and the Foolish Man." Both men are builders and creators; they find a location and begin to build homes. We quickly learn, though, that the foolish man, who was doing his best, built upon the sand, which to him seemed like the ideal place, secure and steady, but the foundation was inadequate. In all the things that we create and build, we must ensure that we have the right foundations in place to make our efforts worthwhile and so that the masterpieces we are creating will stand the tests of time and whatever else might be flung at it.

We should build our homes on the rock—the rock and foundation of our Saviour Jesus Christ and His gospel. Establishing a safe location to build doesn't require qualifications as a surveyor, but we do need to seek the Spirit and follow the teaching of Jesus Christ to get the right spot. The families that we are creating need to include Him and His teachings, and they need to be founded on that. As we nurture and teach those we love about the Gospel and His plan, that foundation needs to be visible in our home for them to anchor to.

Helaman counseled his sons, and this counsel was written down and preserved for us now, as we too needed to be reminded (we are told to remember— twice!).

> And now, my [daughters], remember, remember that it is upon the rock of our Redeemer, who is Christ, the Son of God, that ye must build your foundation; that when the devil shall send forth his mighty winds, yea, his shafts in the whirlwind, yea, when all his hail and his mighty storm shall beat upon you, it shall have no power over you to drag you down to the gulf of misery and endless wo, because of the rock upon which ye are built, which is a sure foundation, a foundation whereon if men build they cannot fall. (Helaman 5:12)

We have talked already so much about this foundation and relationship with our Saviour and Heavenly Parents, but this really does need to be our benchmark when we build, grow, and create. We need to ask ourselves and evaluate whether we are building in a good place with the foundations in the right place and whether we are seeking the advice of the One who knows. We need to not only build but maintain taking custodianship over the things that we are creators of.

Many of us have experienced broken creation or inability to create, be it through infertility, loss of a child, divorce, not being married, death, losing faith, illness, disability, or a million other things that can shatter not only our faith but also our resolve and our hearts. These precious creations. We need to step back a little and look at the creation. Is it something that can be strengthened after this storm? Can it be reinforced and restored, or do we need to start afresh with a clean slate and build bigger and better this time? Do not think that what you built before wasn't good or worthy, that what you were trying to create was a failure; it was all steps on our individual journey. They are a part of what makes us who we are. Some of them will leave painful scars that may never fully heal, but we need to build and create lives and families that will go on and be great despite the mortal challenges and heartaches we may suffer.

Don't ever think you are not a creator; you are. To be able to work hand in hand with your Father and use some of the sacred power of procreation to become a mother is such a special gift and one that I personally wish everyone could have and sail through with ease. But, for some, this is not the case, and my heart hurts for each and every one who suffers this pain. A few years ago my son and daughter-in-law felt that pain; my granddaughter (my first grandchild) was stillborn. She was perfect and beautiful in every way. The most perfect creation of her parents as they endeavoured to build a family. They had suffered infertility, health challenges, and IVF to get this far, and they saw what they were trying to build crash around about them. They were seeking a family and to build a home that was full of love. There is nothing that anyone can say or do to fix this or even to really alleviate the pain. I am grateful, though, that as a woman of great faith, I was able to find great comfort in the knowledge and testimony that I have. I was able to find new resolve to build and work towards the celestial kingdom so that I may be with my granddaughter again. Her parents could now only try to rebuild and reinforce their family and look forward with faith, keeping their precious daughter in their hearts until the time they can hold her again. Her loss was tragic, and she will never be forgotten; however, there was joy to come when eighteen months later they welcomed a beautiful baby boy into the world.

He will never replace our granddaughter, but his creation has brought great joy where there had been great sorrow.

I do believe that all women are mothers and nurturers; although some of our mortal roles might differ, they will not in the eternities. I am grateful for the many women who have mothered and nurtured me, as they each have left their mark and helped me develop my own great faith. We need to make sure, as we build and create, that it is not just ourselves but others too. We can be instrumental in rebuilding and fortifying others as we love and serve them; don't ever underestimate the power we have to influence good in others.

As women of great faith, we need to create and build always, even in the terrible and difficult storms of mortality with the negative influences of the adversary and the natural man. We need to seek ways to not just build great towers but be constantly strengthening and reinforcing. Life can often feel like a Jenga tower; it grows in height, but it becomes more precarious, losing its strength and stability. We need to avoid this, always having the Spirit with us and the strong, sure foundation of the Saviour and the reinforcing power of the Holy Ghost.

Spend time this week checking your foundations and seeing where you are building and creating, where could you build that you maybe haven't, and what storms are on the horizon that you could prepare for.

16
Remember What We Once Knew

"I Lived in Heaven"[99] is a beautiful song that teaches about the premortal life and the plan of salvation. I love this song and how it reminds me, and through song allows me to testify, to share my faith and the knowledge that I have gained as I have grown through mortality, the knowledge of where I came from, Who I lived there with, and that a loving Heavenly Father created a plan for me.

Remembering where we lived before now helps strengthen us and fortify us as we realise that this life is just one small part of our eternal journey. Knowing that we lived before as families and with people we loved tells me all I need to know about the premortal realm: it was home. It also gives me incredible hope in the hard times to know that we will return home one day and be surrounded by those that we love and who love us.

We need to remember that we are women of great faith, as we were in the premortal life. We came together in the heavenly council, where Father presented to us a beautiful plan, one through which we could become more like Him and Mother. He knew it would be hard for each of us and offered a plan, including a Saviour, providing the ability for redemption. Jesus offered that He would take that role. It was exciting, and it was what we all wanted—a body just like Father had—and we wanted to grow and progress. I believe that Father

---

99. *Children's Songbook*, 4.

taught us His plan with great love; He loves and cherishes each one of us, and just as a parent might feel sending a child away on a mission, He and Mother would have been excited but also a little anxious about us leaving Their loving embrace. I believe we, as young spirits, would have been excited, like children (or adults) waiting to go to Disneyland!

We all know what happened next though. Our other brother Lucifer thought that he had a way of improving Father's plan. I want us to just step back and think now about Lucifer. He has become the bad guy and the one we know as Satan or the devil, BUT right at that moment, I wonder whether he was such a bad person. He wanted us all to come home to Father; he didn't want one of us to be lost. He did then, though, let an attitude and emotion come through that we can probably all relate to in mortality. He let what we know as the "natural man" surface. He also missed the most important part and the point of Father's plan—agency, which was critical, because we needed to learn and grow. Otherwise, there was no point in coming here to Earth. So there we have it. Lucifer said he would go but that there would be no agency and we would all come home, but then he showed his arrogance and greed when he wanted all the glory, taking it from the Father. He was rebellious, and I wonder how many of us have felt that way in mortality and how many of us need to recheck that rebellion and establish what it is women of great faith would do!

Therefore, when we study this story and try to remember what we knew, we need to remember that we KNOW we followed the Father; in the war in heaven, we chose the Father and we chose Jesus Christ. Just take that in. We chose Him once, so when we choose Him now again in mortality, it isn't a new decision or a new concept; we are just following through with what we already decided. Women of great faith remember the choices they have already made; they remember the love they have for Father and their big brother Jesus.

We should also remember, though, that there was a war in heaven and that we were a part of it. I am not sure what the war looked like or how long it went on, but as I have thought about it, I can't help but think that it was a war filled with emotions and broken hearts. We talk about living in heaven with people we loved, and I wonder how many of those people we loved chose to follow Lucifer. I wonder if we begged and pleaded with them to come with us and how many of them asked for us to go with them. But, in the end, it was a personal choice, and one in which we accessed our own individual agency, knowing that we would be separated eternally from people who were important to us, even our premortal family. This always makes me think about how we feel now in our mortal families, how many of us have loved ones that we plead with and beg to follow the teachings of Christ and to choose Him as they once did in heaven. Maybe the pain of seeing loved ones move away from the gospel of Jesus Christ and make choices that we know would not be pleasing to the Father makes the veil thin, as we remember the loved ones we lost before in the war in heaven. We need to remember not to make the same mistakes Lucifer made. We cannot take away agency; it is essential to the Father's plan. We can and need to take comfort in His plan; He knows best, and He loves these family members even more than we do! He sent a Saviour for a reason. So we need to remember to take the example of Father, and that is to love—love unconditionally, love fiercely, and love eternally. We still need to invite and set an example and hold fast to our covenants, and as we have talked about before, endure to the end. As women of great faith, we know that it will be okay.

"There will come a day when we will all remember what we knew before we were born. We will remember that we fought in a great conflict for this privilege. How do we meet this responsibility? We daily put our energies into the work that is uniquely ours to do."[100]

The veil was placed across our minds; we can view the veil as a spiritual amnesia. We forgot everything, and the only way we can restore our memory is to keep learning and progressing—learning about the gospel and the scriptures—and then ping! When we read and pray about these things, all of a sudden there are small sparks of memories, and there are glimmers into what we once knew. This will not be fully restored until the end of mortality; however, we can create

100. Julie B. Beck, "Understand the Divine Roles of Women," *Ensign*, Feb. 2009, 67.

small cracks and peek through, and these flashes will be precious to us. When you have these moments when you just know something or feel like you have had these heavenly glimpses, WRITE THEM DOWN. These are things that will help you and your family.

The plan and the truths about life before our birth and mortality bless us with wonderful insights that each one of us needs to remember, and this knowledge builds part of our foundations. But what each of us remembers or our heavenly glimmers and testimony-building experiences will be different. Maybe take some time this week to do a few things. First, think about your knowledge of Father's plan, and ask yourself, *What do I know?* and *What do I want to know?* Then seek out those answers, and study and pray for your own personal revelations. Father sent you here and loves you so much. He is waiting, shielded by the veil, and is longing for us to reach out so that He can comfort us and reassure us. Next, we need to think about what those in our family know and remember about their time in heaven, take time to testify to them, and help them remember.

> In our premortal life, we were taught lessons that prepared us to assist Heavenly Father in bringing about the salvation of His children (see D&C 138:56). We also had the agency to follow and obey God. Some of Father's children distinguished themselves through their "exceeding faith and good works" and were foreordained, or given assignments, to serve in specific ways on earth (Alma 13:3). The greatest of those who followed Heavenly Father back then was His firstborn spirit son, Jesus Christ—or Jehovah, as He was known there.[101]

As women of great faith, we want to remember and act upon the lessons that we were taught and the things that Father prepared us for. How do we know what those things are? We have to talk to Him and ask Him, building a relationship with Him. We can also look to our patriarchal blessings and study them, seeking further and constant revelation from the Father and through the Holy Ghost. He taught you, He prepared you, and He wants you to remember and act upon

101. Norman W. Gardner, "What We Know about Premortal Life," *Liahona*, Feb. 2015.

the revelation you receive. You are one of His secret weapons. Don't forget that!

President Boyd K. Packer taught, "There is no way to make sense out of life without a knowledge of the doctrine of premortal life. ...

When we understand the doctrine of premortal life, then things fit together and make sense."[102]

Much like we cannot remember the first few years of mortal life, our memory of premortal life has been withheld. This was necessary to help us learn to walk by faith and prepare us to become like Him. But we can be assured that we knew and loved our Heavenly Father.

President Ezra Taft Benson (1899–1994) promised that "nothing is going to startle us more when we pass through the veil to the other side than to realize how well we know our Father and how familiar His face is to us."[103]

What an amazing promise, and what a precious day that will be for us as women of great faith when we see Father's smile and know that it is just for us. I like to think that He will embrace us and we will remember our home. It will be the most incredible homecoming.

- How has your understanding of premortal life blessed you?
- What will you do this week to act upon and remember what you know?

---

102. Boyd K. Packer, "The Mystery of Life," *Ensign*, Nov. 1983, 18.

103. Gardner, "Premortal Life."

17
Be a Covenant Keeper

> "There has never been a more important time to understand the power to which we have access because of our covenants than right now! . . . As we live up to our covenants, the angels will not be able to be restrained from being our associates."[104]

Women of great faith are covenant keepers. We seek daily to live up to the covenants that we have made, trying our very best to do our part. I am reminded of goalkeepers when I think about covenant keepers; like them, we stand in protection of our own goal (and goals) as the adversary tries his very hardest to score and get one past us. It is only through constant practice that we will become better and stronger, more able to defend our goal and deflect his advances. Most days, he will get things past us and we will struggle to have a perfectly clean score sheet. But we don't give up; we keep going and trying, reminding ourselves of the why and that we love Father so much and that we really did mean the things we promised; this will give us the motivation to get back up and defend our goal.

As women of great faith, we need to understand and own the power that being a covenant keeper gives us, but we do need to fully understand everything right now! Understanding the power will enable us to expand our faith and realise that we don't have to defend

104. Wendy Watson Nelson, *Covenant Keepers* [Salt Lake City, UT: Deseret Book, 2016], 8, 27.

this goal alone; we have our Saviour and the angels in heaven, who all play on our team. Knowing that angels will not be able to be restrained and will be our associates is incredible. I want them on my team daily, as I am sure you do too! This is an instant reward for keeping my covenants.

Spend a moment now and maybe even write a list of the covenants that you have made with Father, and think about how you might be able to live up to them. We say "live up to them," because they require us to raise ourselves upward toward heaven, not just move forward.

"When we let our covenants influence our thoughts and words and actions, we are inseparably connected to millions of covenant women and men—from the beginning of time down through every gospel dispensation!"[105]

When I think about the wonderful and incredible covenant keepers in my own family, those who have gone before and those whom I have got to know through gospel study, I feel so blessed to know that not only can I be connected to Father and my Saviour Jesus Christ as I keep my covenants, but that they are on my team. Women of great faith who are covenant keepers are never alone; they have a huge and incredible support system. Seek out Father and Jesus Christ and other people as a strength and a beacon.

"Every sister in this Church who has made covenants with the Lord has a divine mandate to help save souls, to lead the women of the world, to strengthen the homes of Zion, and to build the kingdom of God."[106]

Covenant keepers ALWAYS remember Christ; He is a part of their day and every action as they always reflect on what He would do, standing as a witness for Him in all things, on all occasions, and at all times, not afraid to be counted as His. We cannot just be His witness in certain friendship groups or on specific dates; covenant

---

105. Wendy Watson Nelson, *Covenant Keepers*, 42.

106. M. Russell Ballard, "Women of Righteousness," *Ensign*, May 2002.

keepers need to be all in! Covenant keepers serve faithfully, diligently, and willingly because we love Him, and we serve our fellow men and women because they are our eternal brothers and sisters and we know loving them shows love for the Father. This service is lifelong, forever, eternal. Covenant keepers will mourn with those that mourn and be a comfort and a companion during hard times; they are compelled to offer relief. This is one thing I think sisters often excel at. We are the best at giving a hug and a listening ear, we will cry with others and then help them get up, wipe their tears, and continue to fight their battles, standing by their side. Women of great faith are women who take upon themselves the name of Christ, always trying to be His hands and heart in each situation, offering comfort and support as He might; they also take pleasure in ministering to His flock. We need to always be covenant keepers and never leave the goal open.

Why do we make and keep covenants?

> Elder Jeffrey R. Holland explained that "a covenant is a binding spiritual contract, a solemn promise to God our Father that we will live and think and act in a certain way—the way of His Son, the Lord Jesus Christ. In return, the Father, Son, and Holy Ghost promise us the full splendor of eternal life." In that binding contract, the Lord sets the terms and we agree to keep them. Making and keeping our covenants is an expression of our commitment to become like the Savior. (Linda K. Burton, "The Power, Joy, and Love of Covenant Keeping," *Ensign* or *Liahona*, Nov. 2013, 111)

1. Covenant keeping builds, strengthens, empowers, and protects our homes and families. Women of great Faith take great satisfaction in creating homes that teach and nurture the family. They teach of covenants and how it is an honour to be able to keep them.
2. Keeping covenants is essential for true happiness. When we choose to be a covenant keeper and not tick off a list but rejoice and find joy in being able to do as Father would want us to, we will find lasting and empowering happiness. It will be apparent to everyone that you are a woman of great faith, a covenant keeper, and that you are His.
3. Keeping our covenants demonstrates our love for the Saviour and our Father in Heaven. They have kept their covenants to us, and

through His fulfilled promise, Jesus Christ literally gives us everything.

They gave us the world and our families and all that we have, and They have given us eternity. Covenant keepers are humble and can see the Lord's hand and influence in their lives; all of their success and progress they credit to the Father.

"The greatest compliment that can be earned here in this life is to be known as a covenant keeper."[107]

"Our Covenants with God did not start here on this earth, and they will not end here!"[108]

- What covenants have you made?
- Which are you keeping well, and which need work?
- What is the next covenant you will undertake with the Father?

You are a woman of great faith, a fantastic goalie and defender of your covenants. Your covenants are precious to you, and even if you have not kept them as well as you could, Father had a plan for that. We can dust ourselves off, pick back up the metaphorical ball, and throw it far from our goal. We can put things right with the Saviour in our goal.

107. Russell M. Nelson, "Covenants," *Ensign* or *Liahona*, Nov. 2011, 88.

108. Wendy Watson Nelson, "'My Soul Delighteth in the Covenants of the Lord,'" BYU Women's Conference address, Apr. 30, 2015, 6.

18
The Gifts of Women

"The Lord has blessed women with divine attributes of love, compassion, kindness, and charity. Through our visits as [ministers], we have the power to bless each sister as we extend our arms of love and kindness and give the gifts of compassion and charity. No matter what our individual circumstances are, we all have the opportunity to edify and nurture others."[109]

During the Creation man was made. It was apparent to the Father and Jesus Christ that Adam should not be alone, so They created women, as without them, the world was incomplete. I believe that women were not something initially forgotten, but Father loved us so much that He wanted everything perfect before He brought His precious daughters to the earth. It was always the plan, but the time needed to be right. He knew that men could do great things but that women, especially women of great faith, were blessed with a different set of divine attributes. This does not mean that men cannot show love or compassion; it just means that, as women, we are predisposed to be able to fulfil different responsibilities from those of our brethren. We should not seek to be the same; we were created differently for a reason, to be able to create balance. The term used during the Creation of women was *help meet*. "And I, the Lord God, said unto mine Only

109. Silvia H. Allred, "Feed My Sheep," *Ensign* or *Liahona*, Nov. 2007, 113.

Begotten, that it was not good that the man should be alone; wherefore, I will make an help meet for him" (Moses 3:18). On the surface the description *help meet* could almost feel like a lesser character in the story; however, the true meaning is an old and beautiful one that has been lost and certainly misunderstood through time and translations. The Hebrew word for *help meet* is *ezer kenegdo*, which translates to be strong, to rescue and to save, as an equal to our brethren. Just as the right and left hand work in unison to perform tasks, this is also the case with men and women.

We know that He created us for great things and gave us great and wonderful gifts, but what are they? If you sat down now to write a list of your gifts as a woman, what would it say?

The list can be endless and incredible; women are remarkable. David Butler shared with me a story of asking a Young Women's class what God's greatest Creation was; they floundered and were unsure. He marched the girls to the Young Men's classroom and posed the same question, and they answered without delay, "Girls!' I would argue that mankind (both men and women) are His greatest Creation, but as women we struggle to see our greatness and to understand just what amazing strength and ability we have to change the world, starting right here, in our homes and families.

We will now talk about a few gifts. You may not yet have utilised the gift or even realised that you have it yet; we are not all blessed with identical gifts, but we do have them. Take a look at your patriarchal blessing and spot the gifts in there; you will probably find several.

Women have an innate and instinctive inclination to help and comfort those in distress, be it a crying baby or a small child or anyone. We seem to be able to better identify and read body language that helps us realise distress, sadness, or pain in others. Just as our Saviour would comfort and reassure them with words, time, or a hug, women do the same. Who have you comforted today? Did you take time to listen and show the love of Christ to them?

We have the ability to pray, and not just for ourselves but for those in our care and those in need. "Every woman has as certain right to approach the throne of deity in prayer as does any man. I am convinced that our Father in Heaven loves his daughters as much as He loves His sons and that He is as ready to hear their pleas and grant their petitions."[110] We, as sisters, do not have the privilege to administer a sick blessing, but we can access the power of the Father through prayer to help heal and comfort those who are sick or distressed. Have you sought out the Lord in prayer today? Was it mighty prayer, and did you petition the Lord for others? When it comes to prayer, we need to ask, and we need to believe He will answer.

Women of great faith are teachers; we have the beautiful privilege and rights to teach and mould young minds in our homes and families as well as in our callings and assignments. We teach with love. Never underestimate the incredible teacher you are. If you are blessed to be a mother, you will teach your child almost everything that they learn prior to their attending school; you will teach them each and every day whilst they are in your home. The lessons may be academic or practical, they may be by example and by correction, and you will teach about relationships and how to be like Christ. When you have to correct, these are also beautiful teaching moments in which you can mould these young hearts and minds to be mighty. You may be required to teach in this way as a sibling or an aunt, you may have a calling with Primary or other youth, or you may just be able to teach with love for the children in the families you minister to. You are teaching every day, in everything you do. We will also teach our fellow brethren and sisters in our gospel responsibilities and through our actions. What have you taught today? Was it taught with love? And did it bring the student closer to Christ?

Women have the opportunity to proclaim the gospel. My husband could tell you that this is easier for women and specifically me, as I will talk to anyone! He tells me that I wear my heart on my sleeve and seem to manage to get the gospel into almost any conversation. I am not sure that is true; however, I do believe that women have a beautiful gift of communication. Some of us are confident to talk to anyone, whereas some are more confident in their friendship groups. When we speak, do we share the gospel and testify? You are not looking for conversion opportunities, as that isn't the way to have gospel conversations; the way is to live the gospel and not hide it. When you don't drink alcohol with your meal when out with friends, you explain why

---

110. Gordon B. Hinckley, "Ten Gifts from the Lord," *Ensign*, Nov. 1985, 87.

and don't just say you don't drink. When you are attending church, you can say you are and not that you are just unavailable. When you offer comfort, you can tell them that you would like to pray for them. The gospel should be part of who we are, and we should be different, and those around us should be able to see that. By living as an example, proclaiming the gospel should be easy, and those around us will ask questions. That is the beauty; when they ask, you can tell them, and and they feel more inclined to listen! When we are talking to our friends, families, and those we meet about our faith and our convictions, we are testifying in tiny, small moments of normal daily life. We therefore share the gospel in tiny pieces. Don't ever underestimate this powerful gift. Who have you spoken to about the gospel recently? Have you made sure, when opportunities have arisen, that you have taken time to testify?

"Yours is also the privilege to minister in the temples. Women do the vicarious work for women. It is as important that this work be done in behalf of those beyond the veil in the case of women as it is in the case of men. The work you so do is as acceptable to the Lord. It is necessary for the accomplishment of his purposes. It is as spiritually uplifting as is that which men do."[111]

The gifts we can utilise and receive as we serve in the temple are special and sacred; we really are *ezer kenegdo* as we work hand in hand with the brethren and rescue and save our sisters who have passed. When did you last serve in the temple? If you haven't yet been able to serve in the temple, make a goal to attend and realise these gifts.

"God bless you, my beloved sisters. Please know that you are deeply appreciated. Please know that your place in the divine plan is no less important, no less great, and no less necessary than that of men. Paul has said, 'Neither is the man without the woman, neither the woman without the man, in the Lord' (1 Cor. 11:11)."[112]

---

111. Gordon B. Hinckley, "Ten Gifts from the Lord," *Ensign*, Nov. 1985, 88.

112. Gordon B. Hinckley, "Ten Gifts from the Lord," 89.

These are but a few of the gifts that we are given as women. Take time this week to look at your divine gifts; seek them in your patriarchal blessing. Make a list of the gifts you have and use and those you would like to develop. Women of great faith know that they are blessed with these beautiful gifts and embrace them; they seek out ways to grow and develop in the sacred gifts just for them. Women of great faith also embrace that they are *ezer kenegdo* as they seek to rescue and save those within their homes and families.

19

Becoming a Righteous Woman in the Latter Days

"To be a righteous woman is a glorious thing in any age. To be a righteous woman during the winding up scenes on this earth, before the second coming of our Savior, is an especially noble calling. The righteous woman's strength and influence today can be tenfold what it might be in more tranquil times"[113]

The prophets have taken time to specifically speak to the sisters about their incredible roles as righteous women in the latter days and during the "winding up scenes on this earth." I wonder, though, if we, as individuals, have ever examined our role in this. Have we taken on board what they have said, or have we seen it as someone else's responsibility?

What does it mean to be a righteous woman? It means that we must stand up for what is right, stand up for morals and for the gospel. Why have the prophets asked for righteous women, specifically?

"Both a righteous man and a righteous woman are a blessing to all those their lives touch. Remember, in the world before we came here, faithful women were given certain assignments while faithful men were foreordained to certain priesthood tasks.

113. Spencer W. Kimball, "Privileges and Responsibilities of Sisters," *Ensign*, Nov. 1978, 103.

While we do not now remember the particulars, this does not alter the glorious reality of what we once agreed to. . . .

> Let other women pursue heedlessly what they perceive as their selfish interests. You can be a much needed force for love and truth and righteousness on this planet. Let others selfishly pursue false values, but God has given to you the tremendous tasks of *nurturing* families, friends, and neighbors, just as men are to *provide*. But *both* husband and wife are to be parents![114]

What do you think we agreed to before we came here? We can maybe discover some of this as we study our patriarchal blessings and the scriptures and seek answers from the Lord in prayer. What we do know is that we have a part to play and that our part requires that we are righteous; we need to look inward first and strengthen ourselves to stand, but this requires that we are certain of the things that we stand for. Just as on an airplane, we are taught to fit our own oxygen mask before helping others; unless we have our own supply of faith and our connection with Father in place, we won't be as able to help others develop theirs. When we stand, we can change lives, influence the world for good, and we defend the gospel of Jesus Christ and our fellow man and woman. Your role might feel very small, and you may believe that your sphere of influence is just as small and possibly even insignificant, but it isn't.

> Most of the people who've changed my life aren't social media moguls or billionaires or renowned experts. My heroes are people who have taken the time to show me Christlike love and help me understand who I truly am.
>
> Our power as righteous women comes from realizing our own importance, our divine identity, and our capacity for accomplishing many things. In turn, realizing our own worth allows us to help others understand their strengths and their infinite worth as well.[115]

---

114. Spencer W. Kimball, "The Role of Righteous Women," *Ensign*, Nov. 1979, 102–3.

115. Jocelyn Turley, "The Heroic Influence of Righteous Women," *Liahona*, Mar. 2021.

One superpower we have is love—specifically, unconditional or Christlike love. As we learn to develop this and bestow it on our families, friends, and neighbours, our influence and power will be significant. However, the greatest power that a woman of great faith has comes from deep within her soul as she realises and knows who she really is. The more you believe in yourself, your identity as a daughter of a King and a mother in Zion, and as you realise you really are important to Him, the more your power grows; it surges, and your light shines brighter.

When we look around us and at those we love, we would, as a mother hen, like to gather in all our chicks to protect them, but we must let our metaphorical chicks go out into the world. Therefore, we need to protect them with the armour of God, a safety bubble that may help reduce the blows of the world. This armour is forged in our homes through righteousness, scripture study, prayer, and as we teach them to identify the Spirit and to be like our elder brother Jesus Christ. This protection comes from teaching and respecting the laws of morality and chastity as well as the word of wisdom, and it comes from understanding and living up to the covenants that we have made. In bad weather, just as we would remind our child to take with them a coat or umbrella or give them a ride in the car, we should be ensuring that those in our families and those we have custodianship over are spiritually protected with the armour of God as they leave the sanctity of the home. This alone is one of the greatest things we can do as righteous women and women of great faith to strengthen and support our homes and families. Remember this: making your home a place where the armour of God can be forged is one of the MOST important things you can do.

"And now, if your joy will be great with one soul that you have brought unto me into the kingdom of my Father, how great will be your joy if you should bring many souls unto me!" (Doctrine and Covenants 18:16). I used to read this scripture with dread and worry that I wasn't successful as a missionary. One day it struck me, and I began to look at it differently: what if that one soul is me? How great will be my joy then? But how much greater will that joy be if my husband, daughters, sons, and grandchildren are also bought to the kingdom of my Father? Then my extended family, those I minister to, those I am called to serve, and also my friends? I realised that this is a beautiful reminder that I want to be with the Father again and that I have to do my part, but I really don't want to be there without those I love. I hope that as a woman of great faith, I can endure and strive to do everything within my love and power to gather in those I love and help them be protected from the world. That I can stand for them and help them, using my influence for good to help others come back to Father. That I will seek to gather Israel within the four walls of my own home first and foremost.

> Among the real heroines in the world who will come into the Church are women who are more concerned with being righteous than with being selfish. These real heroines have true humility, which places a higher value on integrity than on visibility . . .
>
> Thus it will be that female exemplars of the Church will be a significant force in both the numerical and the spiritual growth of the Church in the last days.[116]

Spencer W. Kimball was talking about you when he prophesied this. This growth is coming through you and me as we show our righteousness and share it in the many ways we are blessed to do so, be it through speech, actions, or the written word. It will be you and me who will help bring this to pass. One powerful tool is social media; we can influence people far and wide. We can share simple and easy things, such as a quote or scripture, but we can also share our testimony in small snippets and recognise the Lord's hand in our lives. We can invite others to come to Christ or just to an activity at church. Be different, be unique, be happy and joyful; don't hide your light but let it burn bright for everyone to see. Never be afraid to be true to yourself and who you are. Make a plan this week to share who you really are on your social media and make your posts positive.

President M. Russell Ballard taught us the following in relation to our status as righteous women:

"Accept it. Understand it. Embrace it. Love it. Share it. Defend it."[117]

---

116. Spencer W. Kimball, "The Role of Righteous Women," 104.

117. M. Russell Ballard, "The Essential Role of Women," *Liahona*, Mar. 2021.

Woman of great faith, you are one of the righteous women that the prophets are seeking; you are the women who are literally changing this world, one day at a time, one person at a time, and as you study this book and embrace who you are, we are excited to see you charge your superpowers and be willing to not just stand but soar!

20
Become Converted

"Sisters, your sphere of influence is a unique sphere—one that cannot be duplicated by men. No one can defend our Savior with any more persuasion or power than can you—the daughters of God who have such inner strength and conviction. The power of the voice of a converted woman is immeasurable, and the Church needs your voices now more than ever."[118]

What does it mean to become converted? We may have also heard the phrase *becoming truly converted*. It is simple, but it is not easy! It means to make a mighty change. I was talking about this with my seventeen-year-old son recently, and he loves to talk in metaphors and said, "So it's a bit like buying a house and converting the loft! The house is now changed; it is bigger and different and always will be." He was right. Our conversion as members of The Church of Jesus Christ of Latter-day Saints often requires renovation and change. We become a member as we are baptised, but the conversion can take much longer. We will need to be knocked about a bit, take away parts, strengthen and change others. We need to strip out the pride, the world, and our natural man (or woman) as we replace them with a stronger foundation on our Lord and Saviour Jesus Christ and a knowledge that all that we have and all that we are is because of His

118. M. Russell Ballard, "Men and Women and Priesthood Power," *Ensign* or *Liahona*, Sept. 2014.

grace. We need to see His hand in our lives and be prepared to stand and do all that He needs of us.

One of the biggest changes we make as we become converted is to set aside our rebellious nature. We will need to make sacrifices and come to the Lord with a broken heart and contrite spirit. We are willing to live by His laws and rules. Becoming converted, or truly converted, could take a whole lifetime, but as we begin on the path to conversion, each day and each step is one closer to who and where we want to be. We know we are becoming converted as we lose our desires for sin and things that can transpire against the Lord's will, when we are filled with love, even unconditional love, and when we desire to share the gospel with others.

Elder David A. Bednar taught us that "Conversion is an offering of self, of love, and of loyalty we give to God."[119]

Just as with our loft conversion, in which we need to add new windows and let in more light, this is also the case as we convert to the Lord. We have to let His light more into our life as we seek truth and knowledge through the scriptures, prayer, and the words spoken by our prophets. We monitor the progress of the loft conversion as we look back to where we were last week or last month, and our spiritual conversion is just the same. We need to always have an eye on the end goal but identify our progress and rejoice in it along the way.

We can learn about becoming converted to the Lord in Mosiah 5:2, which says, "And they all cried with one voice, saying: Yea, we believe all the words which thou hast spoken unto us; and also, we know of their surety and truth, because of the Spirit of the Lord Omnipotent, which has wrought a mighty change in us, or in our hearts, that we have no more disposition to do evil, but to do good continually." Through this conversion, Satan's temptations had no power over the people. How wonderful! What an incredible blessing of conversion that we can reduce Satan's power in our lives.

---

119. David A. Bednar, "Converted unto the Lord," *Ensign* or *Liahona*, Nov. 2012, 107.

As we become converted, we are more conscious of what God and Jesus Christ think of our actions than what others think. We have more strength to make the choices we know to be right and remove ourselves from places where the Spirit cannot dwell.

We will become kinder and more compassionate; we won't judge, criticise, or gossip. We care about how we make others feel and seek out opportunities to serve and help. The Sabbath becomes a delight to us and the best day of the week, a day that we can focus completely on our relationship with the Lord, feeling the Spirit, and serving others. The day that we can renew our covenants and take the holy sacrament.

Our desire to pray increases because we want to be in constant communication with our Father, Jesus Christ, and the Holy Ghost. We pray always and not just when we are in need or distress. We no longer look for excuses or try to push the limits; we simply keep the commandments, avoiding the grey areas.

Knowledge of what is right, through conversion, means that we desire to pay true and honest tithes and offerings; we are joyous in our ability to give to the Lord. We also have a desire and passion to share the gospel because we want others to feel the same joy and happiness that we have found in our conversion.

> True conversion is more than merely having a knowledge of gospel principles and implies even more than just having a testimony of those principles. It is possible to have a testimony of the gospel without living it. Being truly converted means we are acting upon what we believe and allowing it to create "a mighty change in us, or in our hearts." In the booklet *True to the Faith*, we learn that "conversion is a process, not an event. You become converted as a result of . . . righteous efforts to follow the Savior." It takes time, effort, and work...
>
> Living the gospel and standing in holy places is not always easy or comfortable, but I testify that it is worth it! The Lord counseled Emma Smith to "lay aside the things of this world, and seek for the things of a better." I suspect we cannot begin to imagine just how magnificent those "things of a better" world are![120]

120. Bonnie L. Oscarson, "Be Ye Converted," Nov. 2013, 76–7.

Do not be dismayed if you think you are at the beginning of your conversion journey; you are not alone, and each and every day that you strive and endeavour is a day closer. If you have been following this book week by week, you are twenty weeks closer. The desire to become converted propels us along the journey, and very soon you will see subtle changes in your behaviour, and then greater ones. We all need to travel this journey; we will be at different points, and we all need to help one another along, walking side by side with each other and loving one another.

"The Lord wants the members of His Church to be fully converted to His gospel. This is the only sure way to have spiritual safety now and happiness forever."[121]

Women of great faith seek true conversion; they strive to follow the Saviour in all things. We seek spiritual safety and security for ourselves and our families. Like Emma Smith, we put aside the natural man and the ways of the world for greater things. Women of great faith know that the blessings in the future are worth the wait and the work!

> The people we surround ourselves with either raise or lower our standards. They either help us to become the best version of ourselves or encourage us to become lesser versions of ourselves. We become like our friends. No man becomes great on his own. No woman becomes great on her own. The people around them help to make them great. We all need people in our lives who raise our standards, remind us of our essential purpose, and challenge us to become the best version of ourselves.[122]

---

121. Donald L. Hallstrom, "Converted to His Gospel through His Church," *Ensign* or *Liahona*, May 2012, 15.

122. Matthew Kelly, *The Rhythm of Life* [North Palm Beach, FL: Blue Sparrow, 1999], 49.

21
Only a Woman

"Men and women have different gifts, different strengths, and different points of view and inclinations. That is one of the fundamental reasons we need each other. It takes a man and a woman to create a family, and it takes men and women to carry out the work of the Lord."[123]

I want to start by saying men are great. They have incredible roles and do so much to help fulfil the Father's plan; however, there are roles that only a woman can do. Only a woman could have been the mother of Christ; a young and innocent girl who had incredible faith, she was prepared in the premortal realms for this incredible task. This was a role for a woman, and that was the plan; we think sometimes of the men who have played such significant parts in the plan of the Father and the Restoration of the gospel of Jesus Christ, but it is also strewn with incredible, amazing women, women of great faith who have quietly, reverently, and respectfully played their part. The plan of salvation required that Adam would fall "that man might be," and this required that Eve partake of the fruit. It required that baptism would need to be introduced to the earth for our salvation through John the Baptist, which therefore required Elizabeth, filled with great faith, to be his mother, teacher, and parent. The plan also

123. M. Russell Ballard, "Men and Women in the Work of the Lord," *Ensign* or *Liahona*, 48.

required a Saviour, but that meant that it also required Mary, each woman playing a pivotal part in the Father's plan of salvation. The list of women of great faith that are woven into the plan continues, and right here and right now, you are one of those women.

"The Prophet Joseph Smith taught that the Church was not fully organized until the Relief Society had been organized—the priesthood for the men and the Relief Society for the women. He stated, 'I now turn the key in your behalf in the name of the Lord, and this Society shall rejoice, and knowledge and intelligence shall flow down from this time.'"[124]

Have you ever really thought about the fact that you are here, now, for a reason? Have you considered that in Father's plan, you were required right now, today? In the Father's plan, from the very beginning, there were no accidents; He is a planner, and it was in the blueprint for you to be here now! What is it He needs you to do? There is the saying 'Behind every great man there's a great woman', a woman of great faith. There will be so many times in your life when you are the support required for your father, brother, or husband to be able to do everything he needs to. This by no means takes from the importance of your role. Think for a moment about the bishop and the great work he has to do. For him to be able to fulfil his calling, a faithful and strong wife is required to hold the fort at home. The most perfect example of this is our Heavenly Mother; she is needed so that Father can do all He needs to do. She is His *ezer kenegdo*, the left to His right hand.

The term *only a woman* can be misunderstood as a degrading or derogatory term; however, it is the stark opposite: ONLY a woman who can do this work, only a woman who can serve this way. The Lord needs a woman who can magnify and amplify His work in ways the brethren cannot. We don't want to get into a battle of the sexes, as that would disrespect the Father and our brethren; each of us is important in His plan. We are of equal importance to Him, and our ability to progress and our future is tantamount; however, we should

124. Mary Ellen Smoot, "For Such a Time as This," *Ensign*, Nov. 1997, 86.

not confuse this with our roles being the same. We have discussed before that men and women are like a pair of hands and work in unison, with equal potential and responsibility, but our tasks may differ. To open a jar, one hand will hold it still whilst the other one will turn the lid. Is one better or more because it held or turned? No, they are equally important with one another. This is how our tasks as men and women are, and we as women need to look at our roles and responsibilities with the realisation that they are JUST as important as those of the brethren.

The priesthood is one topic where we sometimes can get stuck. Are women lesser because they don't hold it? The answer is no. Are we below or minor in the gospel? NO! The brethren have the responsibility to administer priesthood duties, and we as sisters don't. Although, we must remember that, as sisters, we do have access to all of the power of the priesthood. In callings, in responsibilities, and within the temple, we will use the keys and power of the priesthood as we serve. Each one of us has access daily through our covenants and living righteously. When we are endowed with priesthood power, we are magnified; realising that we have access to this as women enables us to be more than we could be on our own. We are never alone, and have His priesthood power with us always.

"Together we will help prepare the world for the Second Coming of the Lord. I have no question that women, armed with the priesthood power and authority with which they have been set apart and endowed, can fulfill this prophetic vision. May each of us live up to our God-given privileges."[125]

The women we spoke about earlier—Eve, Elizabeth, Mary—and many, many more we could mention understood this power and had great faith and knowledge that ONLY they as women could do what needed to be done. We won't compare men and women but rather explore our own sacred and beautiful roles. We can enjoy and embrace our differences, knowing that we are all traveling on the very same journey, maybe some people in a sports car, some on an open-top bus

125. Barbara Morgan Gardner, *The Priesthood Power of Women* [Salt Lake City, UT: Deseret Book], 137.

enjoying the views, and others in a great big minivan packed with kids and littered with McDonald's fries! The mode of transport doesn't weaken or lessen the role we have as women. You need to realise that, as a woman of great faith, ONLY you can do what the Lord needs done, right here and right now. This is your time, and you are the required piece in the puzzle of our earthy journey. Your worth is incredible and beyond measure.

"There is no number large enough to measure your worth. But there is a number that can determine your destiny. That number is 'one.' We are all 'one' in Jesus Christ."[126]

Because of the one, we are here, we are needed, we are required, and we are capable. We can fulfil our roles and work hand in hand with our brethren doing the things that ONLY we sisters can do. Because of the one, we have access to the incredible powers that enable us, guide us, and protect us. We cannot *just* play our part, but we must do it well, making the difference the Saviour needs us to.

"Sisters, like Esther, *we must prepare for our time because our time has come*. We must possess the spiritual strength to overcome our challenges, laying our faults on the altar and giving our lives to the Lord. We must focus our priorities on contributing, as we are able, to the building of the kingdom of God."[127]

When we study the life of Christ and His ministry, we can see that there were times when ONLY a woman would have been able to do what was needed. We know and understand the role of His precious mother Mary, and the great and many things she did. We know about Mary Magdalene's devotion and faith that she showed as she met Christ by the tomb; she did what was required as she gathered the Apostles, her faith that the Saviour was in fact risen never wavering. Christ surrounded Himself with women of great faith.

126. Dieter F. Uchtdorf, "Young Adult Area Devotional with Elder Uchtdorf," Jan. 9, 2022, YouTube.

127. Smoot, "For Such a Time as This," 87.

> There were other incidents which would indicate a wavering of devotion on the part of his brethren. There was never, on the other hand, time nor occasion when the devotion of the women to the Saviour could have been questioned. The constant affection, loyalty and devotion of the Marys and the other women were evident under every condition.[128]

Let us be like the Marys when we approach our requirements; let us be never wavering women of great and even mighty faith. Let us realise how precious our role is and not compare it to the roles of the brethren as we understand that our roles are sacred and cherished. Let us be like Esther and know that this is our time and this is what we came for. Take to heart the words spoken in *Little Women*: "I'm not afraid of storms, for I'm learning how to sail my ship."[129] Be not afraid. We are learning, and each day we get better and stronger. We are the ONLY women for the job. Let's roll up our sleeves and get to work, doing everything we can to magnify our roles as women.

128. Matthew Cowley, *Matthew Cowley Speaks* (Salt Lake City, UT: Deseret Book, 1954), 320.

129. Louisa May Alcott, *Little Women* (Project Gutenberg, 1996).

22
A Mother in Zion

"A woman with a mother heart has a testimony of the restored gospel, and she teaches the principles of the gospel without equivocation. She is keeping sacred covenants made in holy temples. Her talents and skills are shared unselfishly. She gains as much education as her circumstances will allow, improving her mind and spirit with the desire to teach what she learns to the generations who follow her."[130]

What does it mean to be a mother in Zion? We learn as we study that Zion is defined as "the pure in heart" (Doctrine and Covenants 97:21); it is a collection of righteous people and a sacred place where people are united in cause and one in purpose. We often refer to Zion as our wards and our stakes; it is the Church and a place where we live in righteousness, doing all that we should, and can be the point where heaven meets Earth. Zion is a wonderful place and a destination that should be on all our bucket lists! In the scriptures we read about Enoch and the city where he lived; the city was "called the City of Holiness, even Zion" (Moses 7:19). We are then told that "Zion, in process of time, was taken up into heaven" (Moses 7:21). This was THE most amazing place, and we can hardly comprehend it, as it seems like only a dream, a city without sin where God Himself

130. Julie B Beck, "A Mother Heart," *Ensign* or *Liahona*, May 2005, 75.

could dwell. I think that each of us would love to live there and be surrounded by such magnificence.

So we better understand what or where or how Zion might feel, but if each of us is to be a mother in Zion, what does that mean? I don't believe that the word *mother* here is talking about women who have borne children, as we often might think. The world would tell us that a mother is a woman who gives birth or who has the responsibility of physical and emotional care for specific children, whereas the scriptures teach us that motherhood is an honourable assignment; a mother is worthy of the love and respect of children in their care and the entire community. Maternal instinct is an innate desire to love, care for, and nurture someone or something. This is a sensitive subject for many women who have not been blessed to have posterity during mortality, but each of us is a mother in Zion and has an incredible part to play in God's plan.

> Just as worthy men were foreordained to hold the priesthood in mortality, righteous women were endowed premortally with the privilege of motherhood. Motherhood is more than bearing children, though it is certainly that. It is the essence of who we are as women. It defines our very identity, our divine stature and nature, and the unique traits our Father gave us. . . .
>
> Some women are required to wait to have children . . . But the Lord's timetable for each of us does not negate our nature. Some of us, then, must simply find other ways to mother. And all around us are those who need to be loved and led.[131]

Here, in the Zion that we are building, day by day, brick by metaphorical brick, we are to be mothers; we are to embrace the privilege given to us as women by God, take the gifts that He has given us, and enlarge them. We have the gifts of love, nurturing, and caring—the gifts of mothering—and we can do that for everyone. I have been blessed to have been brought up by a strong and fierce mother. She was a single mum for most of my childhood, and she was much like a lioness. I have felt loved and nurtured by her, and still do as an adult; however, I have also had the blessing of being mothered by many. The influences of my biological mother have made an impact on who I

131. Sheri L. Dew, "Are We Not All Mothers?," *Ensign*, Nov. 2001, 96–7.

am, but so have those of the multitude of mothers who have taken me under their wings and loved me as their own. The words, actions, and care of these great women have etched beautiful lessons into my heart and helped mould the woman I am today. These women have not all been of our faith, but they are great women, incredible examples, and women who embrace their mother hearts. They have influenced how I have chosen to mother, and there have been many who have been blessed as I have taken my turn to mother those who are not biologically my children.

Once I got my own home, I endeavoured to build my own little corner of Zion, one which can be a safety and security from the world. This is not an easy task, and it's a little like trying to build a sandcastle at the beach when the waves keep crashing in and knocking bits down. However, little by little, Zion becomes bigger and better. It will take a lifetime and longer to become what Enoch saw, but it is better than it was yesterday, and that is the plan. I can also assist in the building of Zion within my ward and stake. Within this Zion I can be a mother to EVERYONE; I can love each one of Father's precious children. When we are blessed to be called upon and use our mother hearts in callings, this is a wondrous and beautiful way to mother. I was blessed, for a number of years, to be the Wigan Ward Primary President. I cannot express with enough passion the love I have developed for those within my care. I am able to love and nurture them whilst supporting their families as they build their own little pieces of Zion. I have learned and understand that Father needed me and needed a woman with the gift of a mother heart to perform these sacred roles for Him. I am glad that I have embraced and enlarged my responsibilities and helped build a part of Zion right there in the Primary rooms of our ward. Where are you using your mother heart in your ward or stake right now? Could you let it grow? Could you be doing more to build Zion in your ward or stake?

I have been blessed with many people who have needed mothering and who have come through the doors of our home over the years, and I have tried to love them as our Father and Mother in Heaven do. I have tried to build them and help them establish their own internal Zions, foundations that they can build on. I have been called Mum by hoards of kids that are not mine biologically, and I have been able to nurture children who are struggling, lost, or in pain. These children have not all been members of our faith, but that doesn't matter; they are all God's children who have fallen within my sphere of influence. Being a mum is great, and I am forever grateful that I have had this mortal privilege, but being a mother and loving my wider pool of children has been incredible. It is said that it takes a village to raise a child, and it really does. When we pull together and love in unison as a network of mothers in Zion, we can make Zion the village where these children are raised; we can help make sure not one child in our reach ever feels less than or alone, and we can be the loving arms, gentle word, or cheerleader that child needs (when talking about children, we are talking about children of God, not just infants).

Don't ever underestimate your power and the great and wondrous gift that God has given you of mothering. He gave you the gifts that were possessed by His most precious and beloved, our Heavenly Mother. He knew that you were worthy of those privileges and that you would cherish them. He knew that your heart was big enough to mother the many people who may pass your way and the maternal instincts would be strong within you. He knew that you would endeavour to build a Zion, right here where you are, starting in your home and stretching to the far reaches of your influence.

"You sisters were chosen before the foundation of the world to bear and care for God's children; in doing so, you glorify God (see D&C 132:63)."[132]

Let us, as women of great faith and specifically mothers in Zion, glorify God our Father as we embrace and cherish our gifts of mothering; let us always look to Heavenly Mother as we seek to improve the skills we have. Don't ever underestimate this incredible power. We have often joked in our home that Mum knows everything and that maybe I possess Jedi powers, but I possess powers much stronger and more life-changing than that. I possess the power of a mother heart. Maternal instincts are strong, and the desire to protect is evident. We possess not a sixth sense, but as we accept our role as mothers in Zion

132. Russell M. Nelson, "What Will You Choose?," 19.

and strive in righteousness, we have the gift and power of the Holy Spirit as our constant companion. Most importantly, as women of great faith, we possess the power of love—a real superpower—and this power alone is one that we have seen change the world when we look to our Saviour and His unconditional love for us.

23
We Cannot Delegate, or Can We?

We have all heard, "Why doesn't she learn how to delegate?"

We live in a world where we are taught that delegation is essential for success. It is believed that to be the best, we must learn this life skill and execute it in our daily lives. This can be very true, and as we examine our lives, there will be many things in our work life, callings, and household chores that can be delegated. Women of great faith, or those developing great faith, need this wonderful skill in their armoury.

"Any good leader knows, however, that delegation won't necessarily give him more free time immediately. In the long run, effective delegation *should* give the leader more time for other matters, but in the short time frame, it may involve an even greater time commitment."[133]

We have busy lives that will involve callings in the Lord's Church, and it is an honour and privilege to serve; however, we need to serve to the best of our abilities whilst ensuring that our home and family life isn't negatively impacted. To do this, we need to learn to delegate when appropriate, especially in positions in presidencies. By delegating, we

133. William G. Dyer, "Why, How, and How Not to Delegate," *Ensign*, Aug. 1979.

are able to teach and support others and also enable those we delegate to the ability to serve and grow.

I have always struggled to delegate because I know it is often easier to do things myself and to do them the way I would like, but in doing that, I have seen myself overburdened, burned out, and losing the desire to serve. Many of us will try delegation and then think it's too hard; we get let down, or we decide things are not being done as they should. But when I have been successful, let go, and helped others soar, it has been the greatest blessing to me. I have realised at that moment that I am becoming a little more like my Father and Mother in Heaven.

That said, how can we learn to delegate better?

Pray about it. If you delegate responsibilities in any environment (yes even work!), think through who could be given the responsibility and the exact nature of the assignment. Then seek inspiration.

Don't be afraid to delegate the challenging and meaty assignments; don't just hand out the mundane and keep the greatest growth opportunities for yourself. You may be totally amazed at just how capable another person is. The bigger and more challenging assignments will help others grow, and they really will surprise you. We asked the children to run the Primary presentation in our ward, and as a presidency, we thought they would be able to. Bishop was a little apprehensive, as we said we would not be speaking at all; the children would even conduct the music. We supported them, taught them, and guided them with smaller experiences leading and conducting the opening exercises in Primary. The Sunday of the presentation came, and I felt calm and at ease because I knew they could do it as they overcame shyness and fear. The most timid child, who wouldn't even pray in public, took the lead and was confident and proved herself as totally capable; it surprised everyone, including her parents.

When giving an assignment, we need to ensure that we make clear what the expectations are. Set others up to succeed, with all the relevant information. Ensure that the person knows they have your support and can call on you for help and guidance.

It is important that once you have explained and extended the invitation for someone to take the assignment, you then get a commitment from them. This may require the encouragement and acknowledgment that you believe in them. You can be their cheerleader! With this should also come the understanding of reporting back and letting you know of any challenges.

It's okay to handhold, and this is where it can be hard, as it would have been quicker and easier to do it yourself. However, once we have trained others, how much easier the workload upon ourselves can be! Cooking the family meals is a perfect example of this. When we are asked by others for help, do we allow them to take part in the project and show them, or do we just give the menial task of the boring prep and washing up? Do we take that beautiful moment to show them how to make the sauce or prepare the meat? How fabulous will it be for your children to one day make your favourite meals as a treat for you?

Support, support, support. When we delegate, we cannot just sit back and expect the task to be done; we need to report back regularly and examine what has been done, whether is it going the right way, and what improvements need to be made. I think here of our Father in Heaven and our elder brother Jesus Christ and the Creation, the ultimate example of delegation and teamwork. His example should be what we implement in our daily lives, homes, Church callings, and even work environments. Father is the perfect example. He broke the Creation up into bite-size, achievable, and manageable assignments, the seven days. He then gave instructions and guidelines and let Jesus go and do it. He didn't micromanage, and He offered praise and love when each stage was complete. When the task then required trickier and more difficult parts, Father then came to work alongside Jesus. I love His example, and I am so grateful that we have it available to us.

Although we might outline the assignment and we may detail how things should be done, we must always be full of love and praise for those who have taken upon themselves the task. I follow on social media a lady named Kristina Kuzmic. She was recently asked about chores and whether her children did them. She then showed a video of her son doing one of his chores. He was about ten years old, and he was folding and putting away his laundry. As I watched, I was really struggling because he wasn't folding how I would have, and I wanted to take it from him and say, "No, you need to do it this way," but she didn't; she watched, she thanked him for his help doing the chores, and she praised him for doing it without having to be reminded. She then went on to say that's why her kids do the chores; they are asked, they are appreciated, and they are loved, never chastised or pulled up when they are doing their best. He was really trying, and that is all we can expect. I am not sure if she sneaks in when he isn't looking and refolds the clothes—I would be tempted—but when I considered it, that was a problem for me to overcome and not the person who has fulfilled their assignment. "Sometimes letting things go is an act of far greater power than hanging on."[134] So harness your power, and just let it go!

"Delegation is not just a gimmick to get rid of work. It is a leadership strategy—a larger plan in which the leader is eventually relieved of certain activities and the person receiving tasks experiences growth and development in the new area of work. Effective delegation is the result of Serious planning, a clear explanation of what is involved, proper training, follow-through, and a willingness to let go."[135]

Effective delegation will give us more time for the most important things, those that we cannot and should never delegate. It will teach us leadership and how to be more like our Father in Heaven, and it will help us grow just as much as those to whom we delegate.

We need to remember that Father also gave us assignments and delegated parts of the plan of salvation to us; He gave us specific tasks that we needed to do. He has reminded us of those in our patriarchal blessings and through personal inspiration and revelation. We know He is there for us at any time when we want to seek His support and guidance.

> If we don't do our part, no one else is going to do it for us. … We can't delegate [our part in Heavenly Father's plan of happiness].
>
> We can't pass it off to anyone. It's ours. We can refuse it, we can deny it, but it's still our part, and we're accountable for it. There

---

134. Eckhart Tolle, *A New Earth: Awakening to Your Life's Purpose* (New York, NY: Penguin, 2008).

135. William G. Dyer, "How Not to Delegate."

> will come a day when we will all remember what we knew before we were born. We will remember that we fought in a great conflict for this privilege.
>
> How do we meet this responsibility? We daily put our energies into the work that is uniquely ours to do. (Julie B. Beck, in "Understand the Divine Roles of Women," *Ensign*, Feb. 2009, 67)

Remember that He assigned you a part in this incredible plan because He believes in you; He knows that you can and will do what is needed. He doesn't need to micromanage you, as He trusts you and your decisions. He also knows that you know He is there for you.

As women of great faith, we need to reflect on our abilities to delegate and how we might improve or expand those attributes. We can evaluate our progress and make a list of the things that have been delegated specifically to us and ask ourselves how we are doing with them. Do we need to seek more help and support? We also need to ask ourselves how we can better support those in our sphere of influence to fulfil their assignments.

24
Not of This World

During the time of the Last Supper, Jesus prayed to our Father in Heaven, saying, "I pray not that thou shouldest take them out of the world, but that thou shouldest keep them from the evil. They are not of the world, even as I am not of the world. . . . As thou hast sent me into the world, even so have I also sent them into the world" (John 17:15–18).

We have learned from these passages and been taught many times that we should be "in the world but not of it," but what does that really mean? We live on this beautiful Earth created for us by our Father and our Saviour, placed here to experience all the wondrous things that would help us be more like them. We should love and embrace this world and all of the amazing experiences we can have. We were supposed to thrive as we participated in the many blessings of this world and our mortal experience. How, then, are we to be in it and not of it?

Our Saviour was the perfect example. He lived very much in the world, surrounded by people from all walks of life, including sinners and hypocrites. He was tempted, tried, and ridiculed, but at all times, He was not *of* the world. He was in it every day, and He was invested in it, in the people, and in the places. He was *in* the difficult moments, and He was *in* the joyous and wonderful moments too. We needed to come to Earth to learn and grow, to learn to choose good from evil, and to make good choices. We cannot learn how to avoid and choose against sin if there is no sin around us. It would be like trying to learn to swim on dry land; we must be *in* the water to learn how to swim through it. Being not *of* the world is the important thing. We have already learned that we are daughters of Deity and that celestial glories are what Father has planned for us; we have been designed for greater things. However, this is where we live, and we can keep our eyes heavenward and always look up as we trek through the day-to-day of mortality. Being not *of* it is much like the swimming analogy; we are in the water, in the sea of life, and by swimming, we can control our direction and destination. The tides and currents of adversity will try to pull us in different ways, but as we swim and grow in strength and skills, we will be able to determine our destiny. Being *of* the world is very much like letting the waters take control of everything, floating along to unknown destinations.

My eldest son was a very active child, and keeping him entertained was always a trick! He hated shopping, and when we had to go to town, he would quickly become bored and start to act up. We started to point out interesting things to him at the tops of the buildings, looking at cool statues or gargoyles, and he very soon began to always look up when he was bored. He loved to spy the patterns and designs of the big old buildings that would tower above him. He was there, right in the middle of the shopping street, but he wasn't caught up by the hustle and bustle of the street, because he was looking at arches and windows or shapes in the clouds. This is a little like how we can be in the world but not of it. We have to be here, and we have to navigate the world's busy streets, but we can look up and find beauty wherever we are; we can seek the good in the people or the situation. We can serve and help others, and we can not allow the world to penetrate who we are and where we are going. We can instead be the light in the darkness and the bringer of greatness, even Father's power and influence.

Who we are and what we stand for has an enormous impact on those around us; we are in the world, and we are changing the world. We might not always see it, but our behaviour, attitude, and faith are the greatest tools in Heavenly Father's armoury for these the latter days.

"I wonder if you sisters fully understand the greatness of your gifts and talents and how all of you can achieve the "highest place of honor" in the Church and in the world. One of your unique, precious, and sublime gifts is your femininity, with its natural grace, goodness, and divinity. Femininity is not just lipstick, stylish hairdos, and trendy clothes. It is the divine adornment of humanity. It finds expression in your qualities of your capacity to love, your spirituality, delicacy, radiance, sensitivity, creativity, charm, graciousness, gentleness, dignity, and quiet strength. It is manifest differently in each girl or woman, but each of you possesses it. Femininity is part of your inner beauty."[136]

We can see this coming to fruition with the armies of sister missionaries now serving the Lord in all the corners of His vineyard, but this work isn't exclusively for full-time missionaries; it is for you and me. When we are not afraid to stand as a witness of Christ and discuss our faith and beliefs, we too are missionaries and are playing our part in the great and glorious gathering. When people see that we are different and that we radiate light and kindness, we are forging forward in the work. Where is your light just now? How bright is it? Are you hiding it under a bushel? We are to reflect "articulateness"; this means His work and the fluent and eloquent way we, as women of great faith, should present ourselves and the messages of the gospel of Jesus Christ—in ways that are clear and understandable and with truth. What it means, more than anything, is that we have to open our mouths! We will bear testimony of Christ; this could be in our church meetings or our families, but it will also mean in a million small ways every day. You can testify of Him, open your mouth, and bear witness that you know who you are, where you are going, and what you are becoming and why!

We need to remember:

> *We are not women of the world. We are women of God.* And women of God will be among the greatest heroines of the 21st century. As President Joseph F. Smith proclaimed, it is not for us "to be led by the women of the world; it is for [us] to lead . . . the women of the world, in everything that is praise-worthy."[137]

---

136. James E. Faust, "Womanhood: The Highest Place of Honor," *Ensign*, May 2000, 96.

137. Sheri L. Dew, "We Are Women of God," Nov. 1999, 98.

Have you ever considered yourself a heroine? The hero of the story! Well, you are! In Father's plan, He needed to keep certain spirits back with Him and preserve and prepare them for the latter days, the times when the world we live in would be harder in different ways, with technology and information—both good and bad—at our fingertips and when the adversity and his armies would be holding strategic positions in the battle. He needed strong daughters who would not only be strong enough themselves but also have the ability to reach out and lead and guide their fellow sisters back to the fold.

"Our Heavenly Father has reserved many of His most noble spirits—perhaps, I might say, His finest team—for this final phase. Those noble spirits—those finest players, those heroes—are *you*!"[138]

I want us to think for a minute about this gathering and this role of the heroine. Heroes save; they don't give up. They endure to the end, even when they seem to get knocked off course or when there seems no possible way through. This is much like our responsibilities as ministering sisters, although our role as gatherers is to bring people back to the Saviour, who does the actual saving. How many times has our list of sisters been a daunting prospect and felt like an impossible task? But He knows those sisters in our care and knows that you, right now, are JUST the person they need, the one who can make a difference, even if you haven't actually seen it! We are assigned to nurture, and in doing so, we may never even see the sisters in our care begin to grow or blossom. But that should not stop us. He has tasked us with this and given us a call to arms. Am I my sisters' keeper? I am not sure I would want to pose that question to Father or to our elder brother Jesus Christ, as They would remind us that we are, just as Christ is our keeper.

We are our sisters' keepers; they have been entrusted into our safekeeping. We are to shepherd and love them, and that means knowing them. This is one small way we get to practice being like our Saviour

138. Russell M. Nelson and Wendy W. Nelson, "Hope of Israel," Worldwide Youth Devotional, Jun. 3, 2018.

Jesus Christ. We need to seek the best for them and speak up for them. We need to seek inspiration from Father and then act upon the promptings of what He would have us do for our sisters.

"To follow in the footsteps of the only perfect person who ever lived, we must expect to stretch our souls."[139]

Elder Oaks talks about the courage to speak up, but to speak up with compassion, sometimes in a scary situation, while having a firm conviction of right over wrong, truth over hypocrisy, love over ignorance, hate, and evil. I liked these words from Elder Oaks: "Most people would rather see a sermon than hear one."[140] Yes, I am my sisters' keeper. Are you?

To help us live in the world but not be of it, Sheri Dew said,

> Women of God, that includes us. Tonight I invite each of us to identify at least one thing we can do to come out of the world and come closer to Christ. And then next month, another. And then another. Sisters, this is a call to arms, it's a call to action, a call to arise. A call to arm ourselves with power and with righteousness. A call to rely on the arm of the Lord rather than the arm of flesh. A call to "arise and shine forth, that [our] light may be a standard for the nations" (D&C 115:5). A call to *live* as women of God so that we and our families may return safely home.[141]

You are this woman, you are living in the world and striving every day to be not of it. Women of great faith find ways to daily redirect their course and swim harder and stronger against the currents of the adversary. You have your eyes firmly on the prize of celestial glory, knowing that you were designed for more than this, that Father has much greatness planned out for you. Women of great faith live *in* the world but not *of* it, and they do all that they can to make the world a better place. They serve and love as the Saviour would in difficult and challenging places, and they seek to keep the sisters in their care,

---

139. Dallin H. Oaks, "Brother's Keeper," *Ensign*, Nov. 1986, 20.

140. Dallin H. Oaks, "Brother's Keeper," 23.

141. Dew, "Women of God," 99.

guiding them and encouraging them to swim harder and understand better where they are going.

25
What Will Our Role Be?

Have you ever auditioned for a play or to take part in a musical? Waited and wondered with anticipation for which role you would be asked to play? Or have you been more like me, wishing you had the courage to audition and never thinking that you would be good enough for any of the roles?

The reality is that you are more than good enough for the role for which you have been selected. Maybe we auditioned in the premortal realm, or maybe Father just knew that each of His precious daughters was more than capable of the task and cast each of us in our role. So what is that role? To be a woman of God.

WOW! Do you feel like you have just been given the lead in a show and you cannot sing? You will be aware of my desire to play the piano well, and thirty-eight years since my first lesson, I still have a long way to go. I have played a few times in sacrament (badly) and cringe when I am asked. I know I am the very last resort if they ask, but I say I will and then scream inside, thinking, *What have I done!* I cannot hear the words sung; I block out everyone and everything, including the chorister, which is not appreciated. I play at my speed and spend the entire time wanting to be sick. When I think about my role as a woman of God, it feels very similar. I am filled with doubt and dread at my ability or inability to succeed. Yes, He has endowed us with natural and incredible talents, but as with any role, work is required to become the best and to really embrace and excel.

"No greater recognition can come to you in this world than to be known as a woman of God. No greater status can be conferred upon you than being a daughter of God who experiences true sisterhood, wifehood, and motherhood, or other tasks which influence lives for good."[142]

What does it actually mean to be a woman of God? This phrase doesn't say a *follower* or a *supporter*, although I am sure that both of those play a part; it says *OF God*. When you look into what that means, it could be any or all of the following:

Woman of God literally means that we are *His*, that we are made from Him and He is our Father. Therefore, we are daughters of Deity, daughters of the Almighty. We have within us a part of Him and a part of Heavenly Mother. I remember one of my children once asking if they were therefore demigods, like Hercules. No, we are more than that! Our spiritual parents are god and a goddess, and we have every ability to become just as They are. Our capacity is beyond the understanding of this world; mortal eyes and minds can barely comprehend our potential and our greatness. We belong to Father, not in a possessive and worldly way but in a loving and eternal way. He is our Father and always was and always will be. He loves us now, forever, and always. He is our eternal family. Belonging is a beautiful thing and gives us so much strength. Belonging is never, ever being alone; He is always there.

Being a woman of God means we are like Him; just in the same way we physically and characteristically resemble our mortal parents, we already resemble our spiritual parents. We are like Him and like Her; we have so many attributes through nature and through their nurture that we can depend upon and utilise, as we really do stand as a witness of Him in all times and in all places. Women of God dwell in holy places and make the places where they dwell holy. They are able to seek out the light and shine it round about them for those who are seeking it too, or even to light the way for those who might not yet realise they are looking.

142. Spencer W. Kimball, "The Role of Righteous Women," 102.

Women of God can seek out their siblings here upon the earth to love and cherish as we did premortally. The veil may have shielded our memories of what happened before, but as we love and reach out, we can develop relationships that will spark memories of forever. Just as parents hope and pray that children will love and support one another should they ever be away from them, Father and Mother are relying on us for that. Something as simple as our ministering assignments is just one very small way we get to be women of God and to learn more about and better love our sisters.

Being a woman of God is a privilege, and one we are blessed to know and are beginning to understand. How many people wander the earth without this precious knowledge, not knowing that they are a child of God and they are loved infinitely? I wish I could teach everyone that they are all beautiful, wonderful, unique, and incredible children of a loving Father and Mother in Heaven. Each of us is precious beyond our comprehension, and Father has a plan for us to one day be held once again in His loving embrace. How different would the world be if everyone knew just that? But we do know it, and therefore we, as women of God and women of great faith, need to embrace that knowledge and love everyone just as we know that Father and Mother love them, regardless of circumstances, gender, race, status, colour, sexual orientation, religion, and so on. We can share this love and knowledge with others as we daily work as ambassadors for Father, first in our own homes and families and then in the extended reach of our own personal spheres.

Father knew that He could rely on you and that the love He needs to share is abundant in you. He knew that you would be able to reach those who are precious to Him who have maybe not been able to connect with Him recently, be it through a lack of faith or knowledge. He knew that you would represent Him and that His love and compassion for His children would be strong in you.

Just as becoming a woman of great faith is a process and a journey, understanding and fully embracing our role as women of God can take time and work; some parts come easier than others.

As we become women of God, we seek Him daily and in every moment of life; we read His words and listen to the words of His prophets and the other leaders of His Church. We commune with

God and pray often, even keeping a constant prayer in our hearts. I love to pray all the time; in the everyday moments, I will turn off the radio and chat with Father on my car journeys and even whilst shopping in the store! He always wants to hear from us, about everything.

We will seek guidance and more light in good books and media, we will study our *Come, Follow Me* and try to find the messages left within its pages by our loving Heavenly Parents. We will be more gracious and elevate an attitude of gratitude personally and within our homes, teaching and showing Father's in hand in all things. We will be aware at all times of what we think and what we say, as we know and understand that we are representing Him. When we sing and think of the song "If the Savior Stood Beside Me," we ponder what we would do if He were right beside us. We will ask that of ourselves always in our actions but also our thoughts, each day doing better than we did the day before. We are on our journey, seeking our perfection; we are not there yet and shouldn't beat ourselves up when we stumble or struggle. We must remember that He loves us, He is there, and He knew that this would be hard at times. But His arm is around you, you can cry your tears into His chest, and then we need to remember that He believes in us and knows that we have got this.

We need to expand and develop our compassionate hearts, always seeking others whom we can love and edify, that we can lift and help on their journeys too. We need to try to always seek harmony and make our homes a sanctuary of peace, love, and understanding. Our families need to know that it is a safe place from the world, where they are loved unconditionally, where they can feel peace, and where they can be helped back up to fight another day in the battles of the mortal realm.

Being a woman of God means that we can love even those who may speak maliciously against us and those who might not show us any love at all. This doesn't mean that we don't protect ourselves (Father and Mother don't want us to have a great big target on our back or be constantly pulled down, but They do want us to show love regardless). I have battled with this, and during a particularly difficult time, I chose to metaphorically smother difficult people with kindness. I identified a handful of people (within my ward) who made my life difficult, and I set out on a mission to change their minds about me and to love them so much that they had no choice but to love me back! This was not easy, and I almost gave up several times, but over a number of years, I have been able to chip away at these brothers and sisters and have almost turned each of them and their feelings around. I haven't given up on the others; they are still on my list!

What we need to remember is that we are women of God and women of great faith; we are becoming more each day and each week, little by little, and we are a beautiful work in progress. Just as any masterpiece is made by millions of brush strokes, God's masterpiece of you is underway, and it will be sublime; He sees what you will become and knows of your great worth.

You are His, and He loves you—don't ever forget that, even in the hardest moments. He is there with His hand reaching out just to you so that He can lift you and save you from the daily challenges and trials of mortality. So take each stroke of the brush, one day at a time, doing better and perfecting yourself little by little, knowing that the master artist will make your strokes much more than you ever could alone. Play your part, learn your lines, and embrace this wonderful role that He has gifted to you.

Conclusion: Enjoy to the End!

The words *endure* and *enjoy* have been muddled up before for me; however, on this occasion, there is no accident. We must keep moving forward and daily pull ourselves up and push through the hard days. There will be a light at the end of our tunnel, and sometimes a day or activity we dreaded and wanted to hide from under the duvet will be really enjoyable.

"Because of the loving plan of our Heavenly Father for each of His children, and because of the redeeming life and mission of our Saviour, Jesus Christ, we can—and should—be the most joyful people on earth! Even as the storms of life in an often-troubled world pound upon us, we can cultivate a growing and abiding sense of joy and inner peace because of our hope in Christ and our understanding of our own place in the beautiful plan of happiness."[143]

Knowledge of the plan and our place within it, that it is all for us, and that we have a loving Saviour who will make it right with the Father, should bring us joy every day. We should be joyful people. President Monson said, "Let us relish life as we live it, find joy in the journey, and share our love with friends and family. One day each of us will run out of tomorrows."[144]

We must enjoy to the end and rejoice and find joy in all the small and beautiful parts of mortality. We all have hard things, everyone;

---

143. Patrick Kearon, "Welcome to the Church of Joy," Liahona, Nov. 2024, 36.
144. Thomas S. Monson, "Finding Joy in the Journey," *Ensign* or *Liahona*, Nov. 2008, 86.

even if it seems like people have a perfect and easy life, I assure you that they have their hard going on behind the scenes. We all need a friend to lift us, and in turn, we lift ourselves.

You have made it to the end of the book, and I hope you have enjoyed the journey, but it isn't over. This was the beginning of the new, improved even more, amazing you. I hope you now believe that YOU are important, precious, and exceptional. That our Heavenly Parents are rooting for you to have a mortality that will be packed with joy. I hope you know that you are significant and that your role is paramount in the plan. I hope you have identified a cheer squad of your own who can help you along the way and have maybe joined some cheer squads too.

Woman of great faith, be strong, endure, enjoy, and lean into Him. He will guide you along and help you overcome the obstacles of life. Remember that happiness is an inside job and that you have got this! Get on your tutu and your rain boots and dance around the kitchen being the real, authentic you.

I hope you can lift out this book often and I can cheer you on again. Enjoy the journey, and I hope I get to meet many of you along the road home.

"Do not let your life be like a shooting star, Which lights up the sky for only a brief moment. Let your life be like the sun, Which always burns brightly in the heavens, Bringing light and warmth to all those on earth. Let Your light shine!"[145]

---

145. Matthew Kelly, *The Rhythm of Life* [North Palm Beach, FL: Blue Sparrow, 1999], 9.

About the Author

Michelle is originally from Leicestershire in the English Midlands and currently lives in Lancashire. She is a mum of six amazing people that she is lucky to call her best friends, she is a grandma to a heavenly granddaughter, three grandsons, and another grandchild due soon. She married her best friend thirty years ago, the best decision of her life. She currently serves as a seminary teacher and a bishop's wife. She is a driving force behind the family business—the Latter-day Bookstore England. She loves to travel and cruise around the world on adventures with her family.

She is an author and publisher, initially in the arts and crafts industry, latterly for a Latter-day Saint audience. She is also a games designer—check out It's a Fact: Temples, a game she made for her children and now wants to bless other families' lives with. Michelle has a so-what approach to the gospel and the scriptures, trying to always get to the why and what makes the messages relevant to her today.

She is an advocate for those on the margins of the gospel, and her greatest wish in the world is that people really understood that they are children of a loving Father in Heaven and that HE has a plan for them right here and right now. We are all precious to Him.

Other gospel-related works written or edited by Michelle include:

- *Ministering: Message of Love and Hope* (2023)
- *On the Road to Jericho* (2022)
- *Lenten: 40 Days and 40 Ways to Become More Like Christ* (2021)
- *Adventus: 25 Days, 25 Names & 25 Ways to Come Closer to Christ* (2020)